Beating the Odds

Arthur Levine
Jana Nidiffer

Beating the Odds

How the Poor Get to College

Jossey-Bass Publishers
San Francisco

Substantial discounts on bulk quantities of Jossey-Bass books are available to corporations, professional associations, and other organizations. For details and discount information, contact the special sales department at Jossey-Bass Inc., Publishers. (415) 433–1740; Fax (800) 605–2665.

For sales outside the United States, please contact your local Simon & Schuster International Office.

 Manufactured in the United States of America on Lyons Falls Pathfinder Tradebook. This paper is acid-free and 100 percent totally chlorine-free.

Library of Congress Cataloging-in-Publication Data

Levine, Arthur.
    Beating the odds : how the poor get to college / Arthur Levine and Jana Nidiffer. — 1st ed.
       p. cm. — (The Jossey-Bass higher and adult education series)
    Includes bibliographical references and index.
    ISBN 0-7879-0132-6 (alk. paper)
    1. Socially handicapped—Education (Higher)—United States.
2. Poor—Education (Higher)—United States.   3. Women—Education (Higher)—United States.   4. Universities and colleges—United States—Admission.   I. Nidiffer, Jana, date.   II. Title.
III. Series.
LC4823.L48   1996
371.96'7—dc20
                                          95-9137

FIRST EDITION
HB Printing 10 9 8 7 6 5 4 3 2 1

The Jossey-Bass
Higher and Adult Education Series

• •

To Julie Kidd
with admiration and affection

Contents

Preface

· ·

This is a volume about how poor people get to college. More than is true with most other books, this one results from the people we have gotten to know over the years.

The People in Arthur's Life

My parents, Katherine and Meyer Levine, started me thinking about the question of how young people who grow up in families in which no one has ever before gone to college end up in higher education. My mother graduated from high school; my father dropped out. Twice in his life, my father was offered opportunities to attend college. First, a dentist he worked for as a teenager offered to send my dad to college if he stayed on the job and performed well in school. Then, the G.I. Bill gave him a chance to complete his education as a returning World War II veteran.

Yet from my earliest years, my parents told me I was going to college. It was not so much an order as a fact of life, somewhat akin to hearing we were going to have breakfast tomorrow. I don't ever remember our discussing the subject or questioning its wisdom. College was just something I would do.

My father had an education lecture. I do not remember him giving it to me, but he always gave it to my friends. It seemed interminable. The only part I remember today is that "anybody can be one of the jackasses that pulls the wagon, but in life you want to be the one who drives the jackasses. You can't do that without an education." One of the fears my friends had growing up was getting caught alone in a room with my father. The dreaded education lecture was inevitable, and he continued to give it even after we had finished college. My father would corner my friends who had not gone on to graduate school or had stopped after a master's degree and tell them what fools they were for "dropping out."

I've long wondered where my parents' faith—even unquestioning belief in education—came from. My father died in 1991, and I never got to ask him that question. But I did ask my mother: "No one in our family had ever gone to college; we had no friends who had ever gone to college; my father, a mailman, did not work with anyone who had ever gone to college. Why didn't you tell me to get a job, save money, and buy real estate rather than going to school? How did you know about college?"

My mother nodded and said, "We knew. We just knew."

Another person who gave impulse to this book was Juan. I wondered how he ever made it to higher education. When I was president of Bradford College in Massachusetts, I spent a week living in a low-income housing project. I spoke with dozens of the children and their parents who were living there. They lived in a desolate and rundown place littered with garbage, broken bottles, and old tires. Gunshots rang out several times during my stay. The night was filled with the sounds of drug deals; the kids I spoke with knew where to buy drugs and could tell me the going prices by weight. Prostitutes walked the streets and aggressively hawked their trade.

Most often, the children I met lived with a single mother and a number of siblings. Very few of the mothers had completed high school; many had had their children when they were teenagers, and their children were following the same pattern.

Few of the children knew any world other than the housing project. Most had never been to Boston, thirty miles away. They spoke English poorly, and the majority spoke another language at home. A disturbingly large number of them had fallen at least a grade level behind in elementary school.

Most of the children living in the housing project were destined to drop out before graduating from high school. No one, but no one in the project had been to college or knew anyone who had.

Juan lived in a housing project just like the one I visited. He went to the same schools as the children I had spoken with. The year after I returned from the housing project, Juan was a freshman at Bradford College.

Juan was the recipient of a full scholarship that the college had created for children from housing projects. He and I had long talks. I asked him if it was the scholarship that had brought him to college. Juan said the scholarship made it possible for him to attend college, but with or without it he was determined to go.

Juan changed my thinking. I had been focusing on the obstacles that barred the poor from attending college. Juan shifted my attention to the anomalies, the relatively small number of poor people who actually get to college. He made me want to know what had happened in their lives that made it possible for them to beat the odds.

Julie Kidd, president of the Christian A. Johnson Endeavor Fund, is the final person responsible for this study. Hers is a friendship I have come to treasure over the past decade. Two or three times a year, when I would come to New York City (before moving there permanently in 1994), Julie and I would spend the morning talking. Julie is not an educator by training but by practice and concern. She knows the world of colleges and universities. I have never met anybody more committed to doing what is right. She is a wonderful listener who also asks very hard questions.

Julie is not shy about expressing her opinions, although she is very polite about it. She is both a pragmatist and a dreamer; a thinker as well as a doer. Often, she looks at issues differently than I do and always pushes me in ways that clarify my thinking.

Over the years, we have discussed most aspects of higher education, but we have probably spent more of our time in recent years on issues of higher education and the poor. One day, we were talking about Juan. We hypothesized about what had really made a difference in his life and whether this difference could be duplicated for other poor people. This book came out of that conversation and all the others that followed over the next three years before starting the research.

The People in Jana's Life

Like Arthur, I too am a first-generation college student. Although my parents had only modest amounts of formal education, they sent me a clear message that education was very important.

My father, the son of a coal miner, grew up in a large family that did not stress reading or learning. But my father wanted an education. He told me several stories about the sacrifices of going to school, of walking several miles in the snow, and similar hardships. In fact, to listen to my father, you might think that good weather had not been invented until *after* he was out of school. But he did finish high school while living in South Bend, Indiana, so he enrolled in the local college—the University of Notre Dame. He stayed only a year, though, because it was his bad luck to have graduated from high school in 1929. There had been very little money before the stock-market crash, but there was none afterward. My father had wanted to be a first-generation college student, but he settled for passing that dream on to his children.

My mother's father, on the other hand, was college educated and had worked as a schoolmaster. But his untimely death during the Depression left my grandmother financially struggling. Finishing high school in the mid 1940s, my mother chose to marry and raise a family instead of attending college.

Dad eventually got a job at the local pharmaceuticals company and worked there for the rest of his life. My parents, a factory worker and a secretary (after her last child was born), had middle-class aspirations for their kids but very little money. Dad always made a distinction to me between having no money and being poor: he never wanted us to be poor. For him, being poor meant being without hope. My father's brief encounter with the world of colleges had given him an unquestioning faith in the power of education. He had the dream but not the money. He wanted me to have both.

I don't remember receiving education lectures or explicit "you will go to college" messages, but I always remember associating those ideas with my father. I never aspired to attend a private school; I had no clue even about how to apply to a place like Wellesley. But Dad let me know that the state university was a possibility.

Being a historian by both training and turn of mind, I was also inspired by the stories of students who lived long ago. Arthur and I have been thinking about and studying the various relationships between poor people and higher education for years. We have looked at how poor students get to college today and how they have fared in past eras, how higher education has responded to those students, the founding and growth of colleges specifically designed for the poor, how and what the universities have taught students about the poor, and state and federal education policies vis-à-vis the poor. I always come back to the individual stories.

Most college students in the nineteenth century were from the "comfortable classes," but not all. Diaries and letters of poor students are testimony to the hardships they faced: A young man showed up at Berea College with sixty cents to his name. Three young women appeared at the Tuskegee Institute so poor that they owned one toothbrush among them. A few poor young women attended the newly created state institutions. Like many women of the time, they faced social ostracism and ridicule on campus, but the poor female students could add almost intolerable living conditions to their many other challenges. Their hunger for education, their determination, and their sheer grit have never failed to move me or stir my historical imagination.

Reflecting on our own lives and the lives of those who inspired us prompted us to ask questions about what happens in the lives of people growing up poor that makes it possible for them to go to college. A crucial question then emerged: what can be done to better the odds for poor students?

This book asks how the barrier of poverty can be overcome. It focuses on the success stories—the small percentage of poor people who somehow make it to college. It asks, What has happened in their lives to enable them to beat the odds? How did they come to attend college when their parents had not, when their neighbors had not, and when most of the students at their local schools had not? The aim of the study is to understand the reasons for their success. What factors—relationships, resources, and activities—have made a difference? Is it possible to reproduce those factors and thereby enhance college opportunity and access for other poor people?

Contents

This book is divided into three parts. Part One focuses on the odds against a poor person attending college. In the Prologue and Chapter One, we look at the reality of growing up poor in the United States today and the odds against escaping such poverty. We examine the obstacles posed by poor neighborhoods, poor families, poor schools, and the other social institutions that constitute the life of the poor. We consider the odds against the poor attending college and illustrate in Chapter Two the evolution of our system of higher education with regard to access by the poor. Finally, we look at national higher-education policies and the attempts that have been made to change the odds for the poor.

Part Two is concerned with how poor people beat the odds. Chapter Three describes our study of twenty-four poor, first-generation college students. We then look more closely at the twenty-four students and seek to explain how they, in contrast with their peers, made it to college. In Chapter Four, we look at the most successful of the students—those attending the highly selective university—and identify the factors that made it possible for them to go as far as they did. In contrast, Chapter Five focuses on the group that has had the most difficult experience with higher education— older adults attending community college. So while Chapter Four looks at the ceiling—the combination of factors that make it possible for the poor to go the furthest educationally—Chapter Five looks at the floor—the minimum combination of factors that permit a student to gain access to higher education.

Part Three is concerned with how to improve the odds for poor people. Chapter Six sketches a portrait of nine mentors in the lives of the twenty-four students. We look at where these mentors came from, how they happened to have such strong faith in education, and how they "worked" as mentors. In Chapter Seven, we sum up what we learned from our study. Simply put, what mattered most to the students we studied was the intervention of at least one adult mentor at a crucial time in their lives. The mentors changed the odds. In Chapter Eight, we go beyond our study and look at what we have learned from intervention efforts for poor students in the past. Whether it was a college designed specifically for poor students, financial aid initiatives, transition programs, or comprehensive programs that combined mentoring with financial resources, each undertaking taught us more about what higher-education policy toward the poor should look like to be the most effective.

Acknowledgments

We are grateful to several people who worked with us on this book. Jeanette Cureton conducted several of the interviews of college students in this study. She is a terrific colleague—enthusiastic about the study, creative and deft as an interviewer, and sharp-eyed and critical in analyzing the data. Jane Oleski, who recently completed a master's degree at the Harvard Graduate School of Education, assisted with research on intervention strategies designed to aid poor people in getting to college. She did a first-rate job of chronicling and evaluating programs in operation around the country. Sharon Singleton transformed a pile of yellow legal pads into a manuscript. Beyond providing secretarial assistance, Sharon served as a colleague, offering useful commentary and asking some tough questions. Nancy Bradley and Donna Schroth also helped with the typing; Nancy regularly reported on which portions of the student interviews made her cry. At Teachers College, Nancy Griffing and Kathleen Shin picked up the odds and ends when the project moved from Cambridge to New York, and helped turn the manuscript into a book. We thank all of these people.

We are also grateful to the Christian A. Johnson Endeavor Fund for supporting this project and to the Pew Memorial Trust, which through the Pew Roundtable on Higher Education funded the research in Chapter Two on the historical evolution of access to higher education by the poor.

New York, New York   Arthur Levine
Cambridge, Massachusetts   Jana Nidiffer
September 1995

The Authors

· ·

Arthur Levine is president and professor of education at Teachers College, Columbia University, in New York City. He received his bachelor's degree from Brandeis University and his Ph.D. from State University of New York at Buffalo. Prior to Teachers College, he served as a senior faculty member and chair of the Institute for Educational Management at the Harvard Graduate School of Education.

Mr. Levine is the author of dozens of articles and reviews. His most recent book is *Higher Learning in America*, published in 1993 by Johns Hopkins University Press. Among his other volumes are *Shaping Higher Education's Future: Demographic Realities and Opportunities, 1990–2000* (with Associates), Jossey-Bass, 1989; *When Dreams and Heroes Died: A Portrait of Today's College Student*, Jossey-Bass, 1980; *Handbook on the Undergraduate Curriculum*; *Quest for Common Learning* (with Ernest Boyer) Jossey-Bass, 1978; *Opportunity in Adversity* (with Janice Green) Jossey-Bass, 1985; and *Why Innovation Fails*, SUNY Press, 1980. A 1982 Guggenheim Fellowship winner, Mr. Levine has received other awards as well, including the American Council on Education's Book of the Year award in 1974 (for *Reform of Undergraduate Education*), the Educational Press Association's 1981 and 1989 annual award for writing, and eleven honorary degrees. He is executive editor of *Change* magazine and has served as a consultant to more than 250 colleges and universities. Mr. Levine was also president of Bradford College

(1982–1989) and senior fellow at the Carnegie Foundation and Carnegie Council for Policy Studies in Higher Education (1975–1982).

Jana Nidiffer is currently a visiting assistant professor of higher education at the University of Massachusetts at Amherst. Her areas of specialization include both history and policy. Prior to this position, she taught the history of higher education at the Harvard Graduate School of Education and the University of Massachusetts at Boston. She has also been assistant dean of the college and coordinator of Women's Studies at Brandeis University (1982–1990). Ms. Nidiffer holds undergraduate and master's degrees from Indiana University and a doctorate from the Harvard Graduate School of Education.

   Ms. Nidiffer's research interests focus on how higher education serves previously underserved populations, especially women, as both students and professionals. She is currently preparing a manuscript that traces the development of the first administrative position held by women at coeducational universities—the dean of women. She has also done research on the impact of the curriculum on students and has worked with the New England Resource Center on Higher Education on the General Education Project. She has presented papers on her work at conferences of the History of Education Society and the American Educational Research Association. In 1992 Ms. Nidiffer was awarded the Alice E. Smith Fellowship for women in history.

Prologue

. . . .

Why the Odds Don't Change for the Poor

In 1986, Arthur interviewed more than fifty elementary and junior high school students living in a low-income housing project. He asked them what they wanted to be when they grew up. They answered: firefighter, nurse, secretary, mechanic; only one child named a future occupation that is among the "venerable" professions—doctor. He asked the children whether they thought they would have a chance to do these things. The response was usually "No," or a shrug.

Arthur then asked them what was the furthest they could imagine going in school. The most common answer was tenth grade, followed distantly by the twelfth. The highest educational aspiration for most of these children, then, was to be a high school dropout. Arthur asked them if they knew anyone who had attended college. Their universal answer was "No." He asked whether they knew anyone who had ever completed high school. They named friends of relatives and relatives of friends, but no one in their immediate lives had graduated.

He talked with the children's parents, too, mostly single mothers. He asked them what they wanted for their children. They said the sorts of things parents traditionally say: they wanted their children to be happy, to do well, to be safe, to avoid getting into trouble.

He asked the parents about college. Did they expect their kids to go to college? Their most frequent response was a wide-eyed stare. The prospect was so unlikely as to be unimaginable. It was akin to asking them whether their children would visit Mars this month.

Arthur likened the parents' response to his reaction were someone to ask him if he was planning to buy a yacht. No matter how cheap the price, no matter how good the deal, Arthur would not consider buying a yacht. He had no idea what to do with a yacht. It certainly would not fit into his apartment. Arthur was just not a yacht person. Similarly, these poor parents were not "college people."

Arthur's conversations reflect the national statistics. The poor attend college at far lower rates than do the rest of the population. Students from families in the lowest-income quartile are two and one-half times less likely to enroll in college than are those whose families are in the highest-income quartile. They are eight times less likely to graduate (Mortenson and Wu, 1990, table 1).

The educational disparity between rich and poor has been tenacious. Nearly half a century ago, President Truman's Commission on Higher Education identified five barriers to college for young people. The first was economic. Citing a raft of studies, the 1947 commission stated, "The old, comfortable idea that 'any boy can get a college education who has it in him' simply is not true. Low family income . . . constitutes an almost impassable barrier to college education for many young people. For some, in fact, the barrier is raised so early in life that it prevents them from attending high school even when free public high schools exist near their homes" (President's Commission on Higher Education, 1947, p. 29).

A second barrier, according to the commission, was geography. It found wide differences in both college attendance rates and opportunities to attend college from state to state and between urban and rural areas. At bottom, the commission attributed the variation to socioeconomic conditions, concluding that "regional differences are largely caused by differentials in wealth and human fertility" (p. 29).

The third barrier was race. The commission reported that whites attended college at almost four times the rate of blacks, and it attributed the difference to racial discrimination not only in the South but throughout the country (p. 32).

Religion was the fourth barrier the commission identified. It concluded that "many colleges and universities, especially in their professional schools, maintain a selective quota system for admission" that barred access for Jews and other religious minorities (p. 35).

The final barrier was gender. The commission stated that opportunity for women in higher education was a "relatively recent" phenomenon in the United States (p. 39). But the commission was troubled by the fact that women were losing ground educationally. On the eve of World War II, women constituted 40 percent of all college students; by 1947 they made up only 32 percent. The commission cited statistics showing that the decline was even greater at the graduate level (pp. 39–40).

In one form or another, all five of these barriers continue to exist today. However, since 1947 more substantial progress has been made in eliminating racial, gender, geographical, and religious obstacles to college than in breaking down socioeconomic barriers.

Thomas Mortenson studied college attendance and graduation rates for women, blacks, Hispanics, and the poor during the period 1940 to 1989. Unfortunately, data on Hispanics and the poor were not available until the 1970s. Mortenson found that the barrier of gender had declined dramatically over the period since the President's Commission report. In 1952, after men had returned to the campuses following the end of World War II, a woman between the ages of twenty-five and twenty-nine had a 50 percent lower chance than a man of earning a baccalaureate degree. By the end of Mortenson's study in 1989, the proportion had risen to 96 percent. Stated differently, women represented 48 percent of degrees earned by 1989 (Mortenson, 1991, pp. vii–ix). Interestingly, since the time of Mortenson's study women have become the statistical majority in colleges. Today, women of all ages make up over 56 percent of all undergraduates and earn 54 percent of all bachelor's degrees (*Chronicle of Higher Education Almanac*, September 1994, p. 31).

Attainment by African Americans increased, too, but not nearly as substantially. In 1940, a black person age twenty-five to twenty-nine had 25 percent the likelihood of a comparably aged white person of completing four years of college. By 1989, Mortenson found that the percentage had increased to 52 percent (Mortenson, 1991, p. ix). After a brief decline, the chances of a black student earning a college degree inched up to almost 54 percent of that of whites as of 1993, the last year for which data are available (Mortenson, "Postsecondary Education OPPORTUNITY," November 1993, pp. 2, 6). Of the more than 1.5 million bachelor's and associate degrees earned by American students in 1992, slightly less than 7 percent of them were earned by black students, although blacks make up almost 12 percent of the U.S. population and 16 percent of the nation's twenty-year-olds (*Chronicle of Higher Education Almanac*, p. 31).

Hispanics also closed the gap somewhat prior to 1990, but to an even lesser degree than blacks. In 1973, Hispanics between the ages of twenty-five and twenty-nine had 30 percent the chance of graduating from college of a similarly aged white person. Sixteen years later, the odds had risen 12 percentage points to 42 percent. But according to 1992 U.S. Census Bureau figures, the odds actually fell to 38 percent during the early years of the 1990s (Mortenson, "Postsecondary Education OPPORTUNITY," February 1993, p. 2).

Mortenson's data permit similar comparisons regarding geographical differences. In 1967, a white high school graduate living in the Center City had 84 percent the chance of his or her suburban counterpart of attending college; those living in nonmetropolitan areas had 89 percent the chance. By 1989, the odds for the Center City youngsters had increased to 92 percent, and for nonmetropolitan students they had risen to 90 percent. For blacks, the gains were even larger. Nonmetropolitan and Center City attendance rates actually exceeded the suburban rates for blacks by 1989 (Mortenson, 1991, p. ix).

Geographic differences are close to being erased. However, high school and college graduation rates by region and state continue to vary. For example, the eight states with the highest high school graduation rates are in the nation's heartland, primarily the upper Midwest—Minnesota, North Dakota, Iowa, South Dakota, Nebraska, Montana, Wisconsin, and Kansas. Conversely, seven of the nine states with the lowest graduation rates—Louisiana, Florida, Georgia, Texas, South Carolina, New York, Arizona, Mississippi, and North Carolina—are in the South (Mortenson, "Postsecondary Education OPPORTUNITY," January 1993, p. 3).

In terms of percentage of the population with earned degrees, only 7.9 percent of West Virginia's population have earned bachelor's degrees, but 18 percent of all Colorado residents hold one (*Chronicle of Higher Education Almanac*, p. 6). In the most striking contrast, however, Arkansas has the lowest percentage of its total population (4.02 percent) currently enrolled as students in any degree program, while Rhode Island has almost twice as many students among its residents (7.91 percent). Tellingly, while Arkansas is ranked fiftieth in terms of population enrolled in college, it is ranked fourth in percentage of the population who live below the poverty line, behind only Mississippi, Louisiana, and West Virginia. Not surprisingly, those three states also have relatively small proportions of their populations enrolled in college—4.68, 4.76, and 4.96 percent, respectively (*Chronicle of Higher Education Almanac*, pp. 46–119).

Religious barriers were not examined by Mortenson—and that is in its own way very telling. Overt religious quotas have for the most part disappeared. In fact, in recent years six of the eight Ivy League universities—the institutions most associated with religious quotas historically—have had Jewish presidents.

There is only one group in Mortenson's study for which attendance rates have actually diminished over time, and that is the poor. In 1970, a person from a family in the bottom income quartile had 16 percent the chance of an individual from the top quartile of earning a baccalaureate degree. By 1989, that proportion had fallen to 11 percent (Mortenson, 1991, p. x). As the 1990s progress, the news gets worse: Mortenson updated his findings in September 1993 and noted that the percentage had fallen to below 10 percent. He concluded that "clearly, the affluent are doing extraordinarily well. The same cannot be said for individuals from lesser family incomes. Those from the bottom quartile of family income in particular are faring worse than they have at any time in the twenty-three years of published Current Population Survey data" (Mortenson, "Post-secondary Education OPPORTUNITY," September 1993, p. 7).

The prospects for poor people in the United States are diminishing today. The numbers of the poor are growing. By 1995, there were simply more poor people in this country than there have been in decades. The U.S. Census Bureau reports that in the United States 39.3 million people live below the poverty line, which it defines as an annual income of $14,763 for a family of four. That figure represents over 15 percent of the entire U.S. population. The worse news is that these numbers reflect a growing trend. Poverty is on the rise and is at its highest level since 1961. The story is even more disturbing for children under eighteen. They represent 40 percent of all poor people but make up only 27 percent of the general population. (U.S. Census Bureau, *Current Population Reports*, Series P-60, "Poverty in the U.S.," 1993).

Not only is the number of poor people expanding, but the condition of poverty under which they live is becoming more permanent. The odds of mobility out of the poorest neighborhoods in America are getting slimmer and slimmer. The traditional path to economic mobility in the United States for the poor—education—is becoming less and less accessible. College costs are rising and income inequality between the rich and the poor is growing. For our country's poor, the American Dream is dying.

I

· ·

Weighing the Odds

1

The Odds Against
Escaping from Poverty

In recent years, study after study has shown that the odds against escaping poverty are growing larger. The poor have become more isolated, and the communities in which they reside have grown even poorer. At the same time, the traditional paths out of poverty—following role models, finding jobs, and getting married—have become less accessible (Wilson, 1987; Levine, 1989a).

There are now fewer role models for poor children to follow. With the advent of antidiscrimination laws in housing, professional- and working-class families who had historically been consigned to ethnic and racial ghettos by prejudice migrated in the 1970s and 1980s to higher-income neighborhoods. The result was a rising concentration of poor people in low-income areas and a declining number of economic success models, other than hustlers, drug dealers, pimps, and gang leaders, for children in those areas to observe, much less emulate (Wilson, 1987, pp. 20–62; Levine, 1989a, p. 4).

Jobs also disappeared. Relatively well-paying positions requiring a high school education or less were once available in manufacturing. In the past three decades the number of such jobs in this country has declined precipitously. The consequence has been a labor market requiring more education than most poor people have, a predominance of low-salaried service jobs in poor areas, and much higher than average unemployment rates for the poor, particularly among young people (Wilson, 1987, p. 40; Levine, 1989a, p. 6).

The availability of male marriage partners has dropped as well. At one time, matrimony was considered a path out of poverty for women. Dreams of marrying someone with a brighter economic future were possible; at least there was a chance that a married couple could have two incomes and be better off. However, because of today's higher rates of homicide, incarceration, unemployment, and drug abuse among poor males, that avenue is shrinking. Among the consequences are a growing number of teen pregnancies and a rising tide of poor, female-headed households (Levine, 1989a, p. 3; Levine, 1987, pp. 6–7).

In this chapter, we look at what it is like to live in the United States today if you are very poor. We rely on recent biographies of poor children and a bit of commentary from interviews we have conducted with disadvantaged youngsters over the past decade.

The world that we describe is harsh. In fact, the clearest terminology to explain the reality of daily life in poor neighborhoods comes out of the lexicon of war. The neighborhoods in which poor people live are described—we think without exaggeration—as "war zones." The protective social institutions found in most neighborhoods—churches, youth groups, families, and the rest—are called "bunkers." And the very rare mechanisms in these neighborhoods for finding a way out of poverty are known as "escape routes."

War Zones

Poor communities are coming to increasingly resemble war zones—the domestic equivalent of Bosnia and, until quite recently, Belfast. More and more, they are becoming places in which opportunities are few, violence is high, homicides are commonplace, and mobility out of poverty is less and less likely.

Children born in the poorest areas in the United States face dramatically different futures than do children born to affluence. Arthur compared the prospects of children born on the same day in two bordering cities—one poor, the other middle-class. He found that the children from the poor neighborhood are:

- Twelve times as likely to grow up in poverty.

- Four times as likely to have unemployed parents.

- Six times as likely to live in a single-parent family.

- Seven times as likely to speak English poorly.

- More than three times as likely not to complete high school.

- Twenty times as likely not to graduate from college.

- Four times as likely to be unemployed.

- More than three times as likely to die before reaching adulthood.

Multiplied manyfold, too, is the likelihood of drug abuse, criminal activity, prison, and teen pregnancy (U.S. Census Bureau, 1990).

What the numbers mean is that children born in poverty have a very good chance of remaining poor throughout their lives. The odds are also high that they will grow up in what is now called a "high-risk environment"—a series of conditions that tend to trap kids in a cycle of poverty. These factors include single-parent families, unemployed parents, low family incomes, poor English at home, and violence on the streets. Equally high are their chances of engaging in activities that increase the likelihood of future poverty—teen pregnancy, crime, drug abuse, inadequate education, and jail.

This world of poverty and its impact on young people is painfully illustrated in a book by *Wall Street Journal* reporter Alex Kotlowitz titled *There Are No Children Here* (1988). He wrote an account of two years in the lives of brothers Pharaoh and Lafayette Rivers, who lived in Chicago's Henry Horner housing projects. At the start of Kotlowitz's book, the brothers were nine and twelve years old, respectively.

Pharoah and Lafayette lived with their mother, LaJoe, and had six brothers and sisters. Their three older siblings had each dropped out of school, gotten involved with drugs, and been jailed at least once. Twenty-year-old LaShawn worked periodically as a prostitute to support her drug habit. Paul, nineteen, was in prison for burglary; and seventeen-year-old Terence, who began selling drugs at age eleven, was serving time for armed robbery. The three younger siblings were four-year-old triplets.

LaJoe, who was thirty-five and one of thirteen siblings, moved into the projects at the age of four. She had her first child at fourteen, had the second a year later, and married the father, Paul, when she was sixteen. They remained married, but Paul was a drifter, drug user, and womanizer who came home only sporadically.

At any given time, the people living in the Rivers's apartment were a changing group. The regulars were LaJoe, Pharoah, Lafayette, and the triplets. But LaShawn, her boyfriend, her boyfriend's brother, and her two children were temporary long-term residents. And Paul was also an occasional guest.

It was a tight fit. The apartment consisted of four bedrooms. The mattresses Lafayette and Pharoah slept on were battered and older than the boys. The sparse furniture came from Goodwill. The curtains had two bullet holes in them from stray street shootings. Historically, the principal source of income for the family was welfare.

The Rivers's apartment was part of a high-density housing project—eight blocks containing sixteen high-rise buildings, each from seven to fifteen stories high. Six thousand people lived in the complex; four thousand were children. Forty percent of the apartments were vacant.

The buildings were in bad shape. The mailboxes had been rifled. Hall lights were gone, so residents carried flashlights to see into the hallways. The heating coils needed to warm the building had been stolen, as had the roof fans required for ventilation. Money for paint had run out in the 1970s. The apartment desperately needed repair. The Rivers's apartment had badly worn linoleum, rusted cabinets, leaky plumbing, uncontrollable heat, exposed pipes, stained walls, a horrible stench in the bathroom, and roaches everywhere.

The Horner projects were dangerous, and life in them was violent. During one summer, a person was beaten, shot at, or stabbed every three days. In a week, police confiscated 22 guns and 330 grams of cocaine. Five children were killed during the summer of 1987. And the Horner projects had a violent crime rate twice as high as the city of Chicago's.

For Lafayette and Pharaoh, this world translated into a set of grim realities: their two older brothers in jail, a neighbor accidentally shot, an aunt murdered, a best friend killed, a mother stabbed, and a number of acquaintances wounded or dead. The expectation of violence was a routine part of their everyday life. When shots rang out, as they commonly did, LaJoe and the boys would rush the triplets to the safest part of the apartment building—the hallway floor. If the children were out on the street and heard gunfire, they knew to dive for cover. It had become a matter of reflex. Fearing the worst, LaJoe purchased burial insurance for the two boys and her triplets. As Kotlowitz poignantly noted, "Lafayette and Pharaoh knew of more funerals than weddings" (p. 17).

The Horner projects were dominated by gangs, and the biggest celebrities in the area were gang leaders. For example, one gang, the Conservative Vice Lords, occupied two of the Horner high-rises across the street from the Rivers's apartment. The gang members tore down the cinderblock walls in vacant apartments to provide getaway routes. They controlled a number of renter-occupied apartments as storage areas for drugs and weapons. In one apartment, they kept a machine gun in the underbelly of the refrigerator. They knocked out hallway and entryway lights to defend themselves against police and rival gangs. They guarded the stairwells and posted walking sentries around the projects. They also recruited youngsters, who faced lighter jail sentences, to do the most visible work. One fourteen-year-old, a friend of Lafayette, said he shot and killed an older man in an alley a block from the Rivers's apartment.

It was estimated that the Conservative Vice Lords did a cash business of $50,000 to $100,000 a week.

In short, the Rivers brothers lived in a world characterized by urban decay, frequent and random violence, drugs, failed lives, unemployment, jail, and teen pregnancy. There was only minimal security, little opportunity other than that afforded by gangs, and no obvious way out.

By the conclusion of Kotlowitz's book, Lafayette had become a victim of that world. While Pharaoh, only eleven, was still too young to know what would happen to him, twelve-year-old Lafayette was a sensitive boy who cared deeply about his family and had taken on many of the responsibilities of an adult. He had never experienced the naiveté and carefree existence traditionally associated with youth; rather, from his earliest days he had seen the real and seamy side of life.

By the age of fourteen, Lafayette had been arrested twice, first for shoplifting and a second time (probably falsely) for stealing a car radio. He was wearing gang colors but did not think of himself as a gang member. He had repeated a year of school, missed thirty-five days of class in 1986, and, not surprisingly, had very poor grades. He no longer trusted people. He said, "I don't have friends. Just associates. Friends you can trust" (p. 35). He had little left to believe in. "Everyone and everything was failing him. School. The Public Aid Department. His father. His older brother. The police. And now in a sense himself" (p. 222). He had no plans for the future and no idea what he wanted to be when he grew up. "That seemed too far away" for Lafayette; he "had grown increasingly cynical" (p. 221). And he was angry, saying: "Now it seems like if I get in a fight, I don't care if I kill or something. I don't even care. . . . Someone be telling me in my mind, 'Hurt him, just don't worry about it'" (p. 73).

Lafayette appeared to be on his way to becoming another statistic in the Horner projects, a war zone where lives were lost physically, emotionally, and spiritually in the cross fire every day. It was a place of endings rather than beginnings.

Yet all of the traditional social institutions—family, friends, neighbors, and schools—required for successful adolescent development were present in Lafayette's world. However, each served principally as an extension or mirror of the war zone.

Take Lafayette and Pharaoh's local high school. It mirrored the neighborhood. The school was a quarter-mile south of the projects. It was 93 percent black, and only 40 percent of the students who entered graduated. In a typical term, just 287 of 1,220 students who were enrolled passed all their courses. The violence of the projects was also a fact of life at the school. In the cafeteria, plastic utensils were substituted for metal to reduce the danger of knives, forks, and spoons being used as weapons. In one three-month period, six teachers were attacked by students.

Absentee rates were high. Reading scores and grades were low. Few students graduated, and teacher expectations for students were minimal. Drugs, gangs, and weapons were school fixtures. In this sense, life in the school was not all that different from life on the streets.

One might even say that the Rivers's school was not in the business of preparing students to *overcome* their poverty. Instead, it taught them how to *adapt* to it. It taught the students to accept failure. It taught them that education was not for them. Rather than imparting the skills students needed to one day leave the projects, the schools instead taught them how to survive in that world of drugs, gangs, and weapons.

Pharaoh and Lafayette's family life taught similar lessons. Their father was an alcoholic and a drug user who did not live at home. Their mother was a school dropout. Their older siblings were all drug users. All had been in jail and none had completed school. Their sister worked as a prostitute. Failure in school and society was treated as the norm. Successes were rare, unanticipated, and often snatched away without warning.

Home life for Lafayette and Pharaoh offered no way out of poverty and no real protections from it. The brothers had no successful role models. Instead, they were once again taught to accept failure and were shown how to cope with it through drugs, alcohol, and crime. But in a sense their home and school environments were functional for a war zone—preparing the brothers to take their place on the firing line.

Over the years, we have interviewed scores and scores of youngsters growing up in poor neighborhoods. They have usually described their families, schools, friends, and neighborhoods in ways similar to Pharaoh and Lafayette. Their stories have included talk of alcoholic parents, broken homes, siblings in prison, family drug abuse, life on welfare, loneliness, abandonment, recurrent violence, and death. They described their worlds in harsh terms.

> We lived in low-income housing . . . you had a lot of problems with other houses . . . drug dealers . . . a high crime rate. People stole a lot of cars, burglaries, and things like that.

> People would sell crack on the corner. There were narcotics raids all the time.

> We came from a very poor family, so we didn't have insurance. [As a result, we didn't see a doctor or have medicine when we were sick.] My mother, grandmother, and I lived in one bedroom.

> We would pray for rent, literally. We'd get two months behind in the rent and we'd start praying . . . a lot of times mom and dad had to scrounge . . . borrowing money to feed us.

Like Lafayette and Pharaoh's, most of the relationships in these poor children's lives reflected the war zones in which they lived.

The irony is that most poor kids were not aware of just how troubled their worlds were when they were growing up. One young woman said her neighborhood wasn't bad; in fact, it was pretty good. She then went on to describe widespread drug dealing, gang fighting, killings, robberies, broken families, and intractable poverty. She described a world like the Horner projects.

Studies of young people growing up in real war zones—in places such as Beirut, Belfast, and Vietnam—came to the same conclusions (Rosenblatt, 1983, pp. 15–25). In general, these youngsters took their situations as the norm. They sought ways to try to live a "normal life" in this environment.

Deborah Dwork's study of Jewish children growing up in Nazi Europe, *Children with a Star,* showed the extreme circumstances under which people will continue to behave in this manner. She studied the lives of Jewish children as they were first segregated from the gentile community, then evicted from their homes, subsequently forced to move into ghettos, and finally sent to slave-labor and death camps. Dwork concluded:

> They adapted to the increasingly alien and bizarre world they were forced to inhabit, and they struggled to maintain a certain normality to safeguard basic structures of their pre-war existence: school, the activities of youth, family life, and friendships. As their lives moved away from home toward the final destination, less and less space was allowed to this realm until it disappeared entirely in the camps. Yet the children struggled to preserve it [Dwork, 1991, p. 261].

In a real sense this was what had happened to Pharaoh, Lafayette, and many, many other children who grow up in poverty. They did not recognize how bad and atypical their environment was. They had a vague sense that there was another life, but it was not real to them; it was an abstraction. As a result, they did not attempt to get out of that world. Instead they tried to live a "normal" life within it. Most of the social institutions they encountered assisted them in the process of adjusting.

The changing nature of poverty in America today is enhancing the likelihood that social institutions no longer help people out of the neighborhood but rather help them cope with staying in. The growing isolation of the poor and the increasing concentration of very poor people in low-income areas decreases their contact with other kinds of communities and reduces their knowledge of other life possibilities. The effect is to increase the odds *against* poor people escaping poverty.

Bunkers

Another consequence of the changing nature of poverty is that the social institutions, which once offered a way out of poverty, have grown weaker. They are being overpowered by the war zone and becoming more like bunkers, providing only temporary safety and protection from the onslaught of daily life.

This was well illustrated by veteran *Time* magazine reporter Robert Sam Anson in his book *Best Intentions* (1987). It told the story of Edmund Perry, a seventeen-year-old from New York City's Harlem, who was shot and killed while trying to mug an undercover police officer. While Alex Kotlowitz's book was filled with stories of poor kids dying young and violently on the streets, Anson's account of Edmund Perry's life was different. Edmund was a youngster who seemingly had it made. He had just graduated from one of the most elite preparatory schools in America—Phillips Exeter Academy—and had a full scholarship to Stanford University for the fall semester of 1985. He did not need the money from the mugging, either: he had a summer job at Kidder Peabody that paid $175 a week.

Edmund grew up in a neighborhood like Pharaoh and Lafayette's. Thirty-six five-story tenements lined his street. There were the same gangs, drugs, and shootings that the Rivers brothers experienced. In fact, the drug trade was so blatant in Edmund's neighborhood that the dealers formed an association and asked to use the meeting room at the local grade school for their gatherings. When the principal refused, they protested to the school board and tried to have her fired.

Daily violence was also a given in Edmund's neighborhood. This was so much the case that a friend said, "Edmund died a natural death up here" (Anson, pp. 11, 89).

The local schools Edmund attended were like those of the Rivers brothers, too. Intermediate School 88, the last he attended in Harlem before enrolling at Phillips Exeter, was a crumbling building with metal grates on the lower floors, "giving it the appearance of a maximum-security prison" (p. 43). Security guards patrolling the hallways added to the prisonlike atmosphere. Nonetheless, drug dealing was done out in the open, and four teachers were arrested one year for selling drugs. Test scores, daily attendance, graduation rates, and teacher expectations were as poor as in the Rivers's school. For the most part, the job of teaching meant simply maintaining order.

In addition, Edmund's family was troubled. His father was an alcoholic, and his parents had been separated for several years while he grew up. In short, Edmund Perry lived in a war zone like that of the Rivers brothers. The difference was that he found Phillips Exeter.

His mother, Veronica, had always stressed the importance of education. She had gone to school in Harlem, stayed on to graduate from high school, and wanted to go to college but couldn't afford it. Instead, she married at eighteen. But the college dream never died for her. As an adult, she took night courses at the local community college while working days. Two academic degrees resulted, with better jobs after each. She became a teacher's assistant, was head of the Parent-Teacher Association, and won a slot on the local school board.

She told her children that education was what counted in life. Edmund followed her example. He was the "shining star" of the family and the "crown prince" of his class (p. 89). In eighth grade his teacher recommended him for the "A Better Chance" (ABC) program.

ABC was created in 1963 by twenty-three preparatory schools to increase the number of talented minorities, especially black students, on their campuses. Within seven years, ABC was producing thousands of applications and placing hundreds of black students in private schools. With his high standardized test scores, strong recommendations, and an excellent campus interview, Edmund was admitted in 1980 to Phillips Exeter.

It was dramatically different from any place Edmund had ever been before. With an endowment of $125 million and 880 landscaped acres, Exeter boasted forty major buildings, twenty-three tennis courts, ten baseball diamonds, a football stadium that seated six thousand, two hockey rinks, two pools, a theater, and a quarter-million–volume library. The affluent student body, numbering 980, came from forty-four states and twenty-four countries. The school's number of National Merit Scholars and scores on the College Board exams were among the highest in the nation. Exeter prided itself on educating the leaders of tomorrow.

Academically, Edmund was successful at Exeter. In his junior year, he studied in Spain. When it came time for college, he was accepted to the University of California at Berkeley, the University of Pennsylvania, and Stanford. By any reckoning, Edmund Perry's future seemed assured. No journey he would ever again make in his life would be as long as the one from 114th Street in Harlem to Exeter.

The problem was that Edmund Perry did not fit in anywhere. He did not fit at Exeter because he was too Harlem, too black, too angry, too self-contained, and too cool. He did not fit in in Harlem, either. In the words of an adult who watched Edmund over the years:

He wasn't part of the block any more. Shit, this kid couldn't even play basketball. They ridiculed him for that, they ridiculed him for going away to school, they ridiculed him for being white [p. 205].

A teacher described a conversation with Edmund during his final year at Exeter, a time when he was growing increasingly bitter and isolated:

He [Edmund] said he felt in a way like a hypocrite. Here he was coming on like a kid from Exeter and his true self, the person he really was, was the boy on 114th Street. He didn't know which were going to be his values, Harlem's or Exeter's. . . . It was apparent he was very upset by it—upset to the point where he should have had counseling. I told him he needed it and asked him why he didn't seek it. He said there wasn't anybody on campus he could talk to [p. 151].

A black schoolmate of Edmund's expressed the same feelings:

I can't pretend anymore, changing back and forth, trying to be two different persons. I am not two different persons and I can never be. I'm just one person living in two different worlds. You've always got to remember that, remember who you are, because when you don't, that's when the emergency light goes on [p. 131].

In a way, that was what happened to Edmund Perry: the emergency light came on. He "hadn't figured out how he was going to make it in the world and not leave everything behind. He was always making a choice: one or the other" (p. 203).

On June 12, 1985, Edmund chose to be a street kid from

Harlem; together with an accomplice he mugged an undercover police officer.

The fact is that Exeter should have been a way out for Edmund Perry. But it became only a temporary respite, a bunker, because Edmund had left Harlem only physically. He never departed emotionally or intellectually. And he knew that. When asked about his future by a *New York Times* reporter doing a story on his neighborhood the year before he died, Edmund said, "I'm not out of here yet. I got some to go before I get off 114th Street" (p. 33).

For Edmund, Exeter was an uncomfortable haven from Harlem. It was safe and it did protect him from the violence of the streets and the schools, but it was not real. Even with family support, Exeter was no more than a refuge in Edmund's war zone. Its values, people, and physical plant bore no connection with the real world in which Edmund lived mentally and emotionally. It was something akin to a giant theme park—a place where one goes to visit, not to live.

Previous conversations with poor children have convinced us that many relationships in the lives of disadvantaged children can be bunkers, including families, youth groups, schools, and churches. Often, the children have talked to us about their churches. One young man we interviewed a few years ago described his church as a safety zone of sorts. The worst violence of the neighborhood stopped at its door. Behaviors that were accepted on the block were prohibited in church—like swearing and beating on people. The church was also physically attractive, prettier than anything else in the neighborhood. Moreover, the values the church instilled were a lot better than those that operated on the block; if one followed the church's values, there was the promise of salvation and eternal life. In addition, the church offered a veritable cornucopia of activities. Beyond Sunday services, there was a religious school, youth programs, a choir, celebrations, overnights, and more.

But the reality, according to this youngster, was that the church couldn't really shield itself or its congregation from life in the war zone. For instance, every year the number of pregnant teenagers at services seemed to grow larger. At a nearby church, there was even a gang shooting.

In earlier times, however, churches and institutions like them had offered poor people paths out of their poverty. Books about poor people who made it are replete with accounts of the power of the church. Claude Brown, in his book *Manchild in the Promised Land* (1966), recounts how he found succor in a man of the cloth. Malcolm X was saved by the Muslim religion while in prison (Malcolm X, 1992). Even an institution as seemingly innocuous as the library is credited with helping the poor rise from their poverty; Alfred Kazin in *A Walker in the City* and Kate Simon in *Bronx Primitive* talk about it as a refuge and a vehicle for escape (Kazin, 1951; Simon, 1982).

However, few poor kids find such an institution. And if they do, it is rarely anything other than a bunker, if that. With the growing isolation of poor communities today, these institutions have become far weaker. They are now overshadowed by the more-numerous institutions, such as gangs, that socialize youngsters for remaining in the war zone. Today, the previously helpful institutions are most successful at providing only temporary shelter. They have been devalued.

Escape Routes

As a consequence, paths out of poverty are fewer now than they once were. They are also less visible to the poor, less well trod, and require much more in the way of individual construction.

This is illustrated in another book written by an investigative journalist of a poor kid growing up in the Chicago projects. *Newsweek* reporter Sylvester Monroe told his own story in *Brothers, Black and Poor* (Monroe and Goldman, 1989). Monroe, called Vest by his friends, grew up in the Robert Taylor Projects—two miles consisting of twenty-eight buildings of sixteen stories each that housed nineteen thousand people. He lived in the same world of gangs, crime, broken families, bad schools, and violence as did Pharaoh, Lafayette, and Edmund. Vest too had friends who killed, were killed, and went to jail.

Like Edmund, Vest had a mother who championed education. She told him over and over again that he could be what he wanted to be, but that school was the only way to realize his dreams. Education was "the last best hope for the black man" (p. 6).

Also like Edmund, Vest did well in school. At Wendell Phillips High School, he was a straight-A honors student and track star who devoured books in the school library at the rate of an author a month. He was fondly called "brainiac."

Again like Edmund, Vest Monroe had participated in the ABC program. He left Chicago to attend the all-male Saint George School, a preparatory academy in Newport, Rhode Island. He found the same mismatch between his background and his school that Edmund encountered. Vest quickly decided to leave Saint George and checked into the school's infirmary, where he was told he was suffering from a case of nostalgia. Not knowing what nostalgia meant, he phoned his mother to tell her he had a terrible disease and wanted to come home right away. She said fine, but under one condition: that he had to be shipped home in a box. She later told him it was one of the most painful decisions she had ever made.

This is where the similarities in the biographies of the two young men end. Sylvester Monroe got out of the projects. Unlike Edmund, the road from his prep school didn't lead back home. It took him instead to Harvard University and then into a career as a nationally known journalist.

The path Vest followed was fundamentally different from Edmund's. It was clearer and had fewer forks. Vest knew exactly where he was going. Although his mother never pushed him in any particular direction, he knew from the time he was fourteen years old that he wanted to become a writer, and he never changed course. In contrast, the purpose and direction of Edmund's journey was less certain. His mother was a political activist and a supporter of Malcolm X. Edmund's grandmother had told him:

> I don't want you to come back talking all that white stuff. If you do I'm gonna let you know about it. Don't you ever forget where you came from [Anson, p. 70].

Edmund was charged by his family with the twin goals of remaining true to his past and achieving a traditionally successful future. He never found a path that allowed him to do both. In this sense Vest had a much easier road to follow.

Vest's path was also shorter. The distance between his home and his prep school was not nearly as great psychologically. His position at Saint George was quickly secured. Before he came home for Christmas break, his first return to Chicago, Vest knew he ranked sixth in his class—he was one of the school's best students. His place there was firmly rooted in his academic ability, not his race. He said he did not worry again about whether he belonged at Saint George. Edmund Perry, on the other hand, never had this certainty about his position at Exeter.

Sylvester Monroe was also more secure at home than Edmund was. Vest was popular with his peers. A former gang member, he was even well liked by the gang leaders. In contrast, Edmund Perry was not one of the guys. He wasn't a good ball player by neighborhood standards, and the adults on the block elevated him to a community symbol with sky-high expectations for his achievement. The pressure was incredible. The distances he was expected to cover were enormous.

Sylvester Monroe's path also had trail guides throughout to keep him on course. Both Vest and Edmund had mothers and teachers who supported them, but Monroe also had a teacher at his prep school who eased the transition.

> The first person I met was Gil Burrett, who taught biology and was my faculty advisor. . . . He seemed nice enough to me, extending a warm welcome . . . and helping me get squared away. But something seemed to bother him as he stood there sizing me up for the first time. I had dressed in my best outfit—a wide-brimmed Dunlop hat, dark glasses, Italian knit shirt, reversible baggy pants, brown and white Stacy-Adams wing-tip shoes. . . .
>
> The next day he bought me a blue blazer, two pairs of gray flannel slacks, and a plain pair of black tie shoes. My Stacy-Adams would not do for chapel, he said.
>
> I was thankful for the new duds. They gave me the look of a New England preppie [Monroe and Goldman, pp. 6–7].

For Edmund Perry there was no such person. He felt he could not talk with anyone at Exeter.

This combination of factors—a clear path, a shorter path, and guidance on the path—proved effective for Sylvester Monroe. In the closing sentences of his book, reflecting on a recent reunion with his old friends at the housing project, he explained just how far he had come.

> He felt at home at Trey-nine (his old address), surrounded by old faces and friendships. But he lived in a larger world. Trey-nine was not so much where he belonged as where he was from [p. 270].

He was no longer from the Robert Taylor projects. He had only grown up there. Vest Monroe had found a path out of poverty.

For poor kids like Vest, finding an escape route is a rare event in their communities. Few neighbors, schoolmates, or family members are making the same journey.

The escape routes they followed are usually constructed, not found. Unlike a traveler, who has a map of established roads and can follow the map, the students we spoke to over the years lacked such guides. They behaved more like explorers carving out for themselves the paths they would follow.

In this sense, the escape routes were highly individualized and short-lived paths. Because an individual in a neighborhood, school, or family found an escape route did not mean that a map would be written or passed on, or that the path would be marked for others to follow.

Looking at these realities, Lisbeth Schorr, a student of successful social intervention programs, concluded:

> Early in this century, the routes up and out of poverty were imperfect, and they worked less well for blacks than for whites, but they were plentiful. Most poor and disadvantaged families lived in an environment that provided day-to-day evidence that hard work, ambition, and perseverance brought rewards—reflecting in large part the expanding demands for unskilled labor. Moving up from disadvantage did not require either the personal heroism or intensive help from outside it does now. Today, escape has become harder and happens less often. "It was difficult for me and my generation [to escape the ghetto]," says Claude Brown. "It is almost impossible now" [Schorr, 1988, p. 18].

Put simply, the odds against escaping from poverty are growing larger. The war zones in which many poor people live have become tenacious in holding them there; with their growing isolation, the poor know little about the world outside of poverty—or how to get there. The social institutions that once provided a way up and out of poverty have grown weaker, and many have become only temporary bunkers or respites rather than escape routes. The existing routes out of poverty have diminished in number, and too few poor people know of their existence. The routes must be re-created regularly, poor person by poor person, to keep them from disappearing.

2

The Odds Against
Going to College

*The young man or woman who grows up without a
decent education, in a broken home, in a hostile and
squalid environment, in ill health or in the face of
injustice—that young man or woman is often trapped
in a life of poverty. He does not have the skills
demanded by a complex society. He does not know
how to acquire those skills. He faces a mounting
sense of despair which drains initiative and ambition
and energy.*

Lyndon B. Johnson
Message to Congress
March 16, 1964[1]

*Each year, more than 100,000 high school graduates,
with proved ability, do not enter college because they
cannot afford it. . . . So, we must give every child a
place to sit and a teacher to learn from. Poverty must
not be a bar to learning, and learning must offer an
escape from poverty.*

Lyndon B. Johnson
University of Michigan
May 22, 1964[2]

---

1. Johnson, 1965, p. 376.
2. Johnson, 1965, p. 705.

Between 1867 and 1899, Horatio Alger, Jr. wrote more than one hundred novels about poor boys who rose from rags to riches. The first of the books and the prototype for the genre, *Ragged Dick*, was the tale of Richard Hunter, an orphan who lived on the streets of New York since the age of seven (Alger, 1962). He had acquired many of the vices associated with the streets—drinking, cursing, smoking, and gambling.

However, Dick also had character. He worked hard as a bootblack, a seller of matchbooks, a doer of odd jobs—whatever he could do to earn a living. He never stole. In fact, he went out of his way to do the right thing: recovering a poor immigrant's purloined wallet, bringing change to a customer who had overpaid him, risking his life to save a drowning boy. For his honesty and integrity, Dick was rewarded by several benefactors who gave him a suit of clothes, a gift of several dollars, a job, and most important, advice about how to "prosper and rise up in the world" (p. 108).

Dick followed the advice. He gave up gambling. He opened a bank account. He moved from the streets into a rented room. He engaged a poor boy to tutor him in exchange for sharing his room. He began attending church.

By the end of the book, all of Dick's efforts had paid off. He was hired as a clerk in a counting house. It was an entry-level, white-collar position, the first step in a career in business and finance that provided Dick with a salary far higher than he had ever earned before and that promised a future brighter than he had ever imagined.

The moral of *Ragged Dick* was that in America "poverty in early life is no bar to a man's advancement" (p. 108). With luck, pluck, character, and persistence, fame and fortune were possible for anyone. The specific requirements were piety, hard work, honesty, thrift, abandoning vices, sponsorship, reading, and self-study. Formal education was not essential.

For Americans living between the post–Civil War reconstruction era and World War I, Horatio Alger defined success and the paths by which it could be achieved. His ideas were not new. If anything, they represented nothing more than an update of the aphorisms that Benjamin Franklin had penned nearly a century and a half earlier in *Poor Richard's Almanac*. There was little evidence that Alger's notions were in any way correct; in fact, there was much evidence to the contrary. Yet he offered what America wanted to believe, and between 16 and 17 million (although there were exaggerated claims of up to 200 million) copies of his books were sold before World War I (Mott, 1947, pp. 158–159).

However, by the end of World War II, Alger's world—if it ever really existed—had passed. Schooling and formal education had become prerequisites for success in America; luck, pluck, and character were no longer nearly enough. Changes in the American economy, social structure, and labor force led Harry S. Truman—the last U.S. president not to attend college—to examine the situation. The President's Commission on Higher Education issued its report in 1947 and concluded:

- As the national economy became industrialized and more complex, as production increased and national resources multiplied, the American people came in greater numbers to feel a need of higher education for their children.

- [But] colleges had not kept pace with changing social conditions, . . . [so] the progress of higher education would have to be repatterned . . . to prepare youth to live satisfyingly and effectively in contemporary society.

- American colleges and universities must envision a much larger role for higher education in national life. They can no longer consider themselves merely the instrument for producing an intellectual elite; they must become the means by which every citizen, youth, and adult is enabled and encouraged to carry his education, formal and informal, as far as his native capacities permit [President's Commission on Higher Education, Vol. 1, 1947, pp. 1, 101].

Citing insurmountable barriers to college, the commission found that "[f]or the great majority of our boys and girls, the kind and amount of education they may hope to attend depends not on their own abilities, but on the family and community into which they happen to be born, or worse still, on the color of their skin or the religion of their parents" (President's Commission on Higher Education, Vol. 1, 1947, p. 27). The commission called for a repatterning of American schooling, a broad expansion that would guarantee education for all. Specifically, it recommended high school for all "normal" young people, two years of free college for 49 percent of the population, four years of higher education for 32 percent, and graduate education for perhaps another 13 percent, depending on national need (pp. 37–43). The commission proposed the establishment of "a national system of scholarships . . . and fellowships that will guarantee that a greatly increased number of qualified young people have a chance for full educational development" (p. 22).

Despite periodic legislative forays in this direction, it took almost twenty years for these sentiments to be enacted into public policy. President Lyndon Johnson embraced them as part of his War on Poverty campaign, believing that "the answer to all our national problems" was education (Johnson, 1964). He proposed them as legislation in the Higher Education Act of 1965.

The act included a number of measures designed specifically to assist the poor. There was financial aid, including educational opportunity grants (which were scholarships for "qualified high school students of exceptional financial need"), low-interest loans, and a college work-study program created a year earlier by the Economic Opportunity Act (P.L. 89–239, 1965, p. 14). A variety of teacher-education programs were also developed "to strengthen the educational opportunities available to children in areas having concentrations of low-income families (p. 37). Established as well were educational opportunity centers, intended to identify "qualified youth of exceptional financial need and encourag[e] them to complete secondary school and undertake postsecondary education training, publicize financial aid programs, and encourage dropouts to reenter school" (pp. 17–18). Support was provided for "developing institutions, financially struggling colleges isolated from the main currents of academic life" (p. 11). The intended targets were the historically black colleges and the two-year schools, which disproportionately enrolled disadvantaged students. There was funding, too, for community-service and continuing-education programs, which sought to assist "the people of the United States in the solution of community problems such as housing, poverty" and more (p. 1).

In the years following, the provisions of the Higher Education Act of 1965 were expanded by amendment. Most notable was the creation in 1972 of the Basic Educational Opportunity Grant, now called the Pell grant, which gave aid directly to needy students. It initially provided scholarships of up to $1,400 annually or half the cost of college, whichever was lower, to students from families with incomes below $15,000 per year. Later, the grants grew larger, and the "half the cost" restriction was lifted.

The Higher Education Act and its successor legislation were not the first federal ventures into college financial aid. In fact, much larger efforts preceded it. Between 1935 and 1943, one ingredient of the New Deal's alphabet soup of federal relief agencies was called the National Youth Administration. The program provided work-study jobs to more than 600,000 needy college students at a cost of nearly $93 million (Alterman, 1973, p. 29). More than one out of every eight college students participated, along with 90 percent of all institutions (Levine, D., 1986, pp. 185–209). At the conclusion of World War II, the G.I. Bill (or Servicemen's Readjustment Act of 1944) reached an even larger population—2.2 million former soldiers. The G.I. Bill offered stipends of $50 a month for single G.I.'s and $75 for those with one or more dependents, plus tuition and college costs of up to $500 a term. The total cost for the program between World War II and the Korean War was $14.5 billion

(Alterman, p. 35). In the aftermath of the Soviet launching of the Sputnik satellite in 1958, the National Defense Education Act was also developed; by 1960 it had provided low-interest loans to more than 80,000 students (p. 17).

Each of these acts provided at least some support to needy students. However, what the programs had in common was that they were not antipoverty initiatives. The National Defense Education Act focused on college as a means of competing economically and militarily with the Soviet Union. The G.I. Bill and the National Youth Administration were designed as emergency measures to limit unemployment. None of the programs were intended to open higher education to the poor, nor did any of them emphasize college in and of itself as an instrument for improving the lot of the disadvantaged. Higher education was seen in the G.I. Bill and the National Youth Administration as a holding tank, a vehicle for keeping young people out of the job market in an era of record unemployment. President Franklin Roosevelt caught the mood of the times when he said in 1939, "Just because a boy wants to go to college is no reason we should finance it" (Levine, D., 1986, pp. 216). College was not viewed as a mechanism for breaking the bonds of poverty. What made the Higher Education Act of 1965 unique was that it tied economic progress for the poor directly to college attendance. This landmark piece of legislation established the immutable principle that a college education was a means of breaking the poverty cycle by providing social mobility. With the passage of the initial legislation, access to college by the poor became an explicit element of national policy.

The results of that policy for the poor have been mixed. In the years immediately following the Higher Education Act of 1965, representation of low-income people in college jumped. (Actually, college enrollments in general rose dramatically, spurred on by a combination of distinct events: increased financial aid, a strong job market for graduates, a bumper crop of baby boomers, a rising women's movement, and the threat of the draft.) Between 1965 and 1971, the proportion of college freshmen from families in the bottom income quartile nearly doubled from 12.4 percent to 22.4 percent. The rate of increase was even higher for those from the lowest-income decile. However, in the years since, attendance rates of the poor have roller-coastered. They dropped to 17.6 percent in 1976, hit a high of 24.4 percent in 1981, fell again to 23.2 percent in 1986, and continued to decline slightly through the late 1980s (Davis and Johns, 1989, p. 56–62; Mortenson and Wu, 1990, p. 13).

The bottom line is that the odds of a poor person attending college were better after 1965 than before, but progress slowed quickly thereafter. In fact, the rate of improvement in college attendance since 1971 has been relatively flat for two decades—going up and down but never showing the dramatic increase witnessed between 1965 to 1971. For those among the lowest-income quartile most likely to enroll in college—unmarried eighteen- to twenty-four-year-olds—the odds of enrolling in college since 1970 have varied only slightly—from a little more than 25 percent to a little over 30 percent (Mortenson and Wu, 1990, p. 3). Any way you cut it, the odds are less than one in three that a poor person will attend college—even if he or she manages to graduate from high school—a necessary prerequisite to college that poor kids often fail to complete—and the odds are lower still that a poor student will finish college.

Compared with their wealthier counterparts, this treading of water by the poor actually represents a decline. The purpose of President Johnson's Great Society higher-education legislation was to promote educational equity between rich and poor. During the 1970s, significant progress was made on this agenda. The gap in college attendance rates between the top and bottom income quartiles shrank from 33 percentage points in 1970 to 22 percentage points in 1979. But in the 1980s, the trend moved in exactly the opposite direction, reaching new highs in 1986, when the gap widened to 35 percentage points (p. 6). In short, the equity gains of the 1970s had been erased in the 1980s, and by the early 1990s equity conditions for the poor were as bad as or worse than they had been for more than two decades. In other words, the odds against the poor attending college have been growing larger (Mortenson, "Postsecondary Education OPPORTUNITY," September 1993, p. 7).

Where the Poor Attend College

Not only is being poor a factor in determining whether one goes to college, it is also a determinant of *where* one goes to college. This is a reality that was evident well before the Truman Commission and the Great Society legislation. It started with the very first college in America, Harvard, which made a commitment to educating the poor.

In a curious manner, that commitment has persisted; it has been passed down from institution to institution, from generation to generation of colleges. It has taken on the character of a hand-me-down—a once-cherished cause, later outgrown, no longer wanted, and ultimately given to another in need. In this manner, the responsibility for educating the poor has been passed by wealthy institutions on to less-wealthy schools, from older colleges to their younger counterparts. Throughout collegiate history in this country, the job of educating the poor has been the lot of the newest and least prestigious institutions. As the schools grew older and more prosperous, they gave up the assignment, and their newer, poorer successors accepted it.

There have been a few interesting and important exceptions to this pattern. The American labor colleges, for example, were founded in the early part of the twentieth century specifically to educate the working class. Instead of becoming part of the mainstream of higher education and more expensive—as had the Ivy League universities, the provincial colleges, and the state institutions—labor colleges simply faded away by midcentury. Another exception is the development of the historically black colleges and universities. For the most part, they started out poor and have remained so.

The First Colleges

The typical pattern of how colleges have educated the poor began with Harvard College. In its earliest years, the college's founders proclaimed their intention to open the school to "poor, but hopeful scholars whose parents are not able to comfortably maintain them." And this they did. Although the majority of the first student bodies came from the wealthier and more eminent colonial families, there was also an assortment of poorer families in attendance (Thernstrom, 1986, p. 116; Morison, 1936, p. 102).

To assist these students, as well as to build the fledgling college, scholarship support was raised from within the colonies and abroad. In fact, enough resources were obtained to provide scholarships for between a quarter and a third of the students at seventeenth- and eighteenth-century Harvard. For example, in 1760 sixteen of the forty-nine Harvard undergraduates received aid covering more than half of their tuition, room, and board (Thernstrom, 1986, p. 116).

But this pattern gradually waned. First, the cost of a Harvard education began rising. It increased more than threefold between 1810 and 1860 (Story, 1980, p. 100). By 1840, the cost of attending Harvard was twice that of Yale or Brown (Hawkins, 1972, p. 8).

At the same time, financial aid diminished. In 1723, scholarship and loan support stood at 12 percent of the Harvard budget. By 1781, after a period of stable and then growing enrollment, financial aid had dropped to only 2 percent of the budget (Thernstrom, 1986, p. 116). Fund-raising for scholarships declined sharply as well: prior to 1700, eighteen educational scholarships were created; over the next twenty years, sixteen more were established; but during the following century not a single new scholarship was added. By 1840, only 35 of Harvard's 275 students received any financial support (Thernstrom, 1986, pp. 48, 51).

Opportunities for Harvard students to earn their own tuition money were also reduced. Taking teaching jobs at rural schools during college breaks was one of the most common ways in which students supported themselves. This was made easier by a long vacation hiatus built into the Harvard calendar, but in 1826 the break was eliminated.

Harvard's policy toward the poor during the early nineteenth century was at best ambivalent. In 1826, a board of overseers committee declared that "Harvard was not designed by the Founders to be an establishment for the rich alone." They feared that, given the rising costs, others would be unable to send their children to Harvard (Thernstrom, 1986, p. 119). A year later, the same committee proclaimed that the college should not exhaust its resources for the support of a large number of indigent persons. "If not invited to the university, [the poor] might become useful and respectable in some other course of life" (p. 120).

The student body at Harvard changed accordingly. Contemporary observers painted a picture of an institution in transition, with increasing numbers of students from "rich and fashionable families" (Story, 1980 p. 91). Or as another put it, "[A]s poorer students have ceased to enter Harvard classes, these were filled in large proportion by the sons of wealthy persons" (p. 91). One 1849 commentator noted that the vast majority of undergraduates were "the sons of wealthy parents . . . [whose] standard of expense, in regard to dress, pocket money, furniture, etc. . . . renders it almost a hopeless matter for the young man of slight means to obtain an education at Harvard" (Lipset and Riesman, 1975, p. 79). By the early 1870s, at least half of Harvard's undergraduates could afford a servant, and 84 percent had fathers who were professionals or businessmen (Thernstrom, 1986, p. 124).

In the years since, this percentage has risen slowly, while the proportion with low-income parents—laborers and farmers—has continued to decline. A study by Seymour Martin Lipset and David

Riesman (1975) put it this way: "[T]he statistical evidence clearly shows that Harvard has been and still is a college for children of business and professional families" (p. 100).

The New Liberal Arts Colleges

With these changes in Harvard and comparable changes at the other colonial colleges, the task of educating the poor fell increasingly to a new generation of schools created between 1769 and 1822. They were rural, they were religious, and they had little in the way of resources. They were Brown, Dartmouth, Williams, Middlebury, the University of Vermont, Bowdoin, Colby, Mount Holyoke, and Amherst. In fact, Amherst was specifically created as a charity school to provide "a classical education [to] indigent young men of piety and talents for the Christian Ministry" (King, 1950, p. 10).

These new provincial colleges were greeted, in the words of historian David Allmendinger, with an "invasion [of] indigents and paupers," (Allmendinger, 1975, p. 12). Students came from the farms and hilltops in the antebellum years, a time when opportunities in agriculture were few, as land had grown less productive and the population had mushroomed. The students wanted training for the ministry in an era of religious fervor and broadscale revivals, and they would not have gone to Harvard because they considered it too liberal—and not jokingly called it "Godless Cambridge." They could not afford to go in any case. They sought colleges closer to home.

In the antebellum years, about one-third of the students attending these provincial colleges were poor—nearly three times the rate at Harvard or Yale. But some of the new colleges were even poorer than their provincial counterparts. In 1829, for example, more than half the students at Bowdoin could be classified as indigent (p. 12).

At Dartmouth, a majority of students were from farm families of limited financial circumstances (Tobias, 1982, p. 59). A member of the class of 1850 described his fellow students:

> They were not born in the purple of affluence or reared on the rainbow promise of great expectations. . . . Reared on small sabine farms, they were inured to the discipline and hardship of stated labors. And better still, many of our boys knew what poverty meant. They had faced its hard conditions and experienced the weight of its pinched pressure. . . . Right well did they know the value of a college education that had cost them so much in labor and self-denial [p. 59].

Amherst was similar. Edward Herrick, a member of the class of 1859, put it this way: "Amherst was poor. There were few students here from wealthy families—one or two perhaps upon every row of benches in the old Greek room" (Herrick, p. 10).

Though life for the poor student was difficult, these new colleges made a good education possible. Their tuition rates were low. Financial aid, though very limited, was creatively used and consisted of small grants, loans, and cancellation of charges. Amherst placed its entire endowment into a charity fund. Williams reduced tuition an average of two-thirds for poor students (Allmendinger, 1975, pp. 50–51). Acceptance of payment in kind—coal, animals, produce— was common. The calendar provided a three-month winter break to allow students to take jobs. Student housing was built austerely to reduce cost. As a Williams student of 1818 wrote, "[N]o room had a carpet, only one room had blinds, and not half a dozen were painted. . . . We all made our own fires and took entire care of our room . . . most of us sawed our own wood" (p. 87).

Moreover, students at Amherst and Middlebury were permitted to live and eat off campus. This made it possible to find even cheaper housing and food. Foraging in the forest and hunting for meat were quite popular as well among the poor scholars. At the older colleges, students were required by charter, as an integral part of college life, to live and dine together in the commons. This more expensive approach to college education was not abolished until 1825 at Harvard. In contrast, Bowdoin, Brown, and Dartmouth had eliminated the practice at least a decade earlier (p. 84).

A few early examples of women's education also fit the pattern. Beginning with academies and seminaries in the 1820s and 1830s, college for women was largely the province of middle-class and wealthy families, but there were exceptions. Mary Lyon, who founded Mount Holyoke in 1837, made her college accessible to poor women. She was able to charge a tuition that was two-thirds less than that of other comparable institutions by assigning domestic chores to *all* students and faculty (Solomon, 1985, p. 24). The increasingly feminized profession of teaching gave poor women an option to work that was becoming less and less available to men at wealthier institutions such as Harvard, which had eliminated the long winter breaks when teaching jobs were plentiful.

Yet, as with Harvard earlier, the new colleges began to change over time, and they changed in precisely the manner that Harvard had. Many women's colleges, for example, had become elite and expensive by the twentieth century, following the pattern set in an earlier era by liberal arts colleges for men. Williams College is exemplary of what occurred.

Enrollment at Williams had risen substantially, from 119 students in 1836 to 240 in 1859. However, financial aid expenditure remained nearly constant. In 1836, tuition and fees were $33, and the total financial aid available was $800—approximately $7 per student, or 24 percent of tuition and fees. By 1868, the cost had risen to $51, while total financial aid expenditures were only $900 for more than twice as many students. This amounted to less than $4 per student, or 8 percent of tuition and fees—a precipitous decline over four decades (Rudolph, 1956, pp. 68–69).

The cost of living on campus also increased substantially over the period: between 1836 and 1866, dormitory prices doubled. Rooms had become far more comfortable and accordingly more expensive. The effect was to drive poor students off campus. In 1840, 18 percent of Williams students lived in town. Twenty years later the proportion had risen to 47 percent (p. 69).

The student body at Williams grew more national. The last year in which most Williams students came from Massachusetts was 1844; by 1871 two and one-half times as many came from New York. The rural origins of the student body of 1836 had given way to an influx from the major cities by 1871 (p. 69). Indeed, as early as 1861 Samuel Armstrong described the Williams students as "smart, fine, and polished fellows" (p. 66). The transformation was rather remarkable. A 1927 study found that 68 percent of Williams students at that time had parental incomes of more than $10,000. By contrast, this was true of only 47 percent of Yale's undergraduates (Reynolds, 1927, pp. 23–24). Historian Frederick Rudolph described the change this way:

> Unquestionably what had been in 1836 a college for poor aspiring clergymen had become, by 1872, an institution strongly marked by wealth, fashion, city manners, and all the other requirements for worldly success [Rudolph, p. 72].

The State Colleges and Universities

And so it was that once again the job of educating the poor became the task of another group of institutions. Now it had become the lot of the state colleges and universities.

Public higher education was born in the nineteenth century. Its roots were several: state colleges, the first of which disputably was created in Georgia in 1785; municipal institutions such as the Free Academy (now City College of New York), established in 1846; normal schools for educating teachers, developed first in Massachusetts in 1837; agricultural colleges like Maine's Gardner Lyceum, which opened in 1821 to train farmers; and a host of schools spawned or upgraded by the Federal Land Grant of 1862 for the purpose of educating students in agricultural and mechanical sciences, as well as in the liberal arts.

With the exception of the municipal colleges, these institutions tended to be located in small towns or rural areas some distance from the established Eastern colleges. They boomed in the Midwest and the West, particularly in the years following the Civil War.

A large number of students who attended these schools were the children of farmers, particularly at the non-Eastern colleges. Institutional records of parents' occupations or income levels are sketchy, but all evidence suggests that many students came from families that eked out a "meager living" (Carey, 1977, p. 66).

The normal schools, which enrolled 16 percent of all college students in 1870 and 30 percent in 1900, were among the poorest (Clifford and Guthrie, 1988, p. 57). Their students were in many ways reminiscent of the earliest undergraduates at Williams, Dartmouth, and Amherst. They were older—over twenty-six years of age on average when they graduated (Harper, 1935, p. 102)—and more than half were children of subsistence farmers, widows, or young people without resources (p. 100). In 1874, one student described himself and his classmates:

> We were shabbily dressed in those days. I think my pantaloons were generally too short and my coat seemed to have been made for some other person. We were very poor, but very plucky. We boarded ourselves on corn-mush, washed the floors and built fires at Normal Hall; worked hard, lived hard and were poorly provided with all things [p. 101].

A Bloomington, Indiana, newspaper put it simply: "The Normal is predominantly the school of the farmer and the poor man" (pp. 100–101). This was a fact of life for the normal school that never changed, and it was still true half a century later when a national survey by E. O. Reynolds concluded that students at normal schools "came from homes of lower socioeconomic levels than students of our colleges or universities" (Reynolds, 1927, p. 24). Indeed, sixteen times as many normal students had unskilled laborers for fathers, and fewer than half as many had fathers who worked as businessmen or professionals (p. 17).

The new public colleges responded to their students in the same manner as the provincial schools had: they kept tuition low. For example, the University of Michigan initially had no tuition. Anyone who could afford to board in Ann Arbor was permitted to attend (Peckham, 1967, p. 1). Similarly, when Indiana became a state in 1816, a provision was written into its constitution that "[i]t should be the duty of the general assembly, as soon as circumstances will permit, to provide by law a general system of education . . . from township school to state university, wherein tuition should be gratis, and equally open to all." When Indiana University was founded in 1820, the tuition was not quite gratis, but as late as 1828 it was as little as $5 per term. Students short of cash offered goods such as bacon, potatoes, corn, butter, or raccoon skins in barter (Harding, 1904, p. 20).

Beyond tuition, costs at the public colleges were kept to a minimum. One historian described life in Ann Arbor in 1847 in the following way: "The boys led a Spartan existence. They paid $7.50 a term for their room, $2.50 for incidentals, and another $1.25 to $1.50 for firewood—which they had to split in the adjoining woodyard and carry up to their rooms. They also carried up water from the pump for washing and furnished their own candles" In addition, the boys took care of the rooms, sweeping out their own dirt and ashes (Peckham, 1967, pp. 22–23).

Life at the University of Wisconsin was similar. Tuition was $10 per year and room and board was $2 a week. In the 1850s, the chancellor of the university remarked, "No educational institution in the country 'offers the advantages of liberal culture on more favorable terms'" (Curti and Carstensen, 1949, p. 86). However, the poorest students were forced to further cut corners on their food expenses and "board themselves" rather than pay the university room and board fees. Many lived on bread and milk and the fish they could catch in nearby waters. One impecunious student noted in his diary in 1861 that he was once able to afford the "rare treat" of potatoes (p. 189). Another student—future naturalist John Muir—struck up a friendship with a janitor who tended the wood furnace so that he could boil "his mush on the coals and bake his potatoes in the hot ashes" (p. 190). Poor students were known to "batch it" on a diet of crackers and prunes (Slosson, 1910, p. 194). If students roomed on campus, they furnished their quarters by any means possible, including liberating the straw needed for a mattress from nearby farms (Curti and Carstensen, 1949, p. 188).

As at the provincial colleges, students were permitted, and often forced, to live off campus to reduce expenses. Students at the University of North Dakota lived in "squalid little room(s) downtown" (Geiger, 1958, p. 37). At the Univesity of Minnesota in Minneapolis, students lived above wagon shops or stores in rooms with only a "bedstead and a straw tick" (Gray, 1951, p. 48). At Indiana University, students pooled resources to buy collectively and reduced the cost of weekly board by nearly half (Harding, 1904, p. 62). Some Kansas State students had their clothes shipped from New England in missionary boxes (Carey, 1977, p. 66).

Stories of hardship and sacrifice by poor students were legion. Like their brothers, poor women in state colleges and normal schools worked to minimize expenses but had the additional burden of fewer employment opportunities and less freedom to pursue unusual living arrangements. A remarkable young woman, Mamie Alexander Boyd, described her experiences at Kansas State in her autobiography, *Rode a Heifer Calf Through College*. To finance her education, she sold a beloved heifer calf for $17.50. That was her only capital for four years. She used boxes for furniture and scrimped on food. She also survived tuberculosis, although her roommate died in her arms of the disease (Carey, 1977, p. 88).

Students also managed to keep the costs of extracurricular life to a minimum. At the University of North Dakota, "[A]musements were simple. The young men and women, many from isolated and primitive farms, enjoyed each other's company at meals, in class, or in supervised 'socials' of games, songs, and talk in the public parlor. A literary society, Adelphi, offered a combination of fellowship, literary discussions, and oratory. . . . Church was a diversion" (Geiger, 1958, pp. 38–39).

There were also opportunities to work. In general, college calendars were designed to allow students extended periods in which to take jobs and earn money. The universities of Maine, Cornell, Minnesota, and Wisconsin, as well as other land-grant colleges, used the university-owned farms and agricultural stations as sources of employment for male students. At the University of Minnesota, wages ranged from five to fifteen cents an hour (Smith, 1972, p. 42; Curti and Carstensen, 1949, p. 94).

However, like their predecessors, the public colleges changed over time. The late nineteenth century was an era of university building, when institutions such as Harvard and Wisconsin grew from colleges into research universities. Beginning in 1819, expanding numbers of Americans desiring advanced education would travel to Germany to study at the great research universities. They returned converts. During the antebellum period, experiment after experiment was conducted—mostly unsuccessfully—to develop a research university in America, or at least to make the American college more of a place for scholarship. The turning point came in the years following the Civil War. A model research school, Johns Hopkins University, was created in Baltimore in 1876. Graduate programs were organized. The award of the Ph.D. degree spread. Colleges were becoming universities.

The public institutions followed suit. Some, like the universities of Wisconsin and Michigan, were leaders. Freestanding agricultural schools became units of larger universities. Normal schools were both merged into universities and transformed into colleges that offered a fuller range of collegiate courses of study in addition to teacher preparation. In 1900, there were 331 normals; by 1928 there were only 69 (Clifford and Guthrie, 1988, p. 57). A normal school became a state college for the first time in 1903; three decades later, 109 had made the change (Pangburn, 1932, pp. 121–122).

With these developments, both the cost to the student and the price of educating students at state colleges and universities rose. In 1895, tuition hikes at the University of Wisconsin brought protests (Curti and Carstensen, 1949, pp. 452–453). Eight years later, when the Kansas legislature raised university fees to $9 per year, the increase—"felt in the pocketbooks" of many students—was staggering to poor undergraduates (Carey, 1977, p. 88).

Life on campus became more expensive as well. During the 1910s and 1920s, public institutions built more dormitories and began requiring students, at least freshmen, to live in them. This left students with few low-cost housing options. Even if undergraduates were allowed to board off campus, landlords in college towns raised the prices to offset the loss of revenue created by the dorms (Breed, 1909, p. 62). Room and board at the University of Wisconsin, for example, was as high as $7 a week before 1900 (Curti and Carstensen, 1949, p. 663).

Poor students were also increasingly excluded from college life at public institutions as Greek societies grew in prominence. Fraternities brought "social cleavage" to most campuses, and some were notorious for their lavish lifestyles (p. 666). Because fraternity members controlled most other aspects of the extracurricular life, students excluded by finances or social undesirability remained on the margins of the college scene. The student body became less homogeneous and differences in wealth more noticeable.

By 1920, the nation's state colleges and universities were increasingly becoming middle-class institutions, as a ballooning proportion of young people sought admission into higher education. Children of upper- and middle-class families replaced the poor students on state university campuses, although these institutions remained

more diverse in student background than were their historical predecessors. Indeed, a Depression-era study of parental occupations of
students at the University of Minnesota found 1 student for every
21 professionals in the state, 1 for every 185 clerical workers, and
only 1 for every 1,583 laborers. The results were comparable in
Kansas in the 1940s: the student body divided into parental occupation showed 3.2 professionals' children, 2.55 proprietors' children,
1.29 clerical workers' children, 0.78 skilled workers' children, and
0.16 children of unskilled laborers (Levine, D., 1986, p. 130). Or
stated differently, for every 320 students who were the children of
professionals, only 16 other students on campus were the children
of unskilled laborers.

Historian David Levine (1986) concluded that "though the state
universities permitted greater access to higher education, the children from less privileged socioeconomic backgrounds were still ter-
ribly underrepresented there" (p. 130). In fact, as early as 1927 a
national study showed state universities looking increasingly like
their historical predecessors, underrepresented by children from
poorer families and overrepresented by wealthier families compared
with the nation's public schools (Reynolds, 1927, pp. 12, 14).

Community Colleges

With these changes, the two-year college took on the job of educating the nation's poor. During the first few decades of the twentieth century, two-year colleges grew in number. Like the state
institutions, the soon to be known as community colleges were a
product of the age of the university. Not only was the university
looming as a superstructure above the college, but the expanding
high school was pushing from below, in effect squeezing the college
at both ends. University leaders such as Henry Tappan at Michigan,
David Starr Jordan at Stanford, and Nicholas Murray Butler at
Columbia had hoped the old-time version of college might dis-
appear altogether, with the high school assuming the function of

the first two years of college and the university embracing the final two years.

William Rainey Harper, the president of the University of Chicago, took the first steps toward realizing this plan. In 1896, he divided his undergraduate college into two units, which he called the junior and senior colleges. Four years later, Harper convinced the Chicago faculty and trustees to award a new degree, the associate of arts, for students who completed the junior college. His plan was for many, and perhaps most, junior college students to accept the associate degree as a terminal degree rather than going on to university study. Harper also prodded the local high schools, encouraging them to extend their programs through the fourteenth year of schooling, incorporating the lower division of college. The principal of the nearby Joliet, Illinois, schools took Harper up on the offer. The University of Chicago in turn promised to grant Joliet graduates upper-division standing. In 1901, a new institution, Joliet Junior College, was created—the first freestanding two-year program in the country (Brint and Karabel, 1989, p. 25).

In 1906, at the age of forty-nine, Harper died before he could bring his plan to fruition. The legacy of his effort, however, is that the president of one of the wealthiest and most prestigious universities in the United States became the father of the two-year college.

Harper's progeny mushroomed. By 1920, there were more than 200 two-year colleges (Cohen and Brawer, 1982, pp. 10–11). Their programs prepared students principally for upper-division transfer to a university by preparing students in the liberal arts. Less than a quarter of the course offerings were vocational.

Two out of three of the junior colleges were private. There was a remarkable difference between the public and private sectors (Koos, 1925, p. 158): while the public two-year colleges were much less expensive ($263 per year on average) than public mainstream colleges and universities ($455), the private two-year colleges were more costly ($690) than either (p. 147). The student bodies varied accordingly. Those attending the private junior colleges came from families nearly as wealthy as those with children studying at the old-est and most elite universities in the country. Their public coun-terparts, by contrast, were more than twice as likely to have parents who were manual workers (p. 158).

In the years between the two world wars, the junior college movement accelerated. While state colleges were accepting a wealthier group of students, the number of two-year institutions rose by a factor of nearly three. Almost half of all new colleges in Amer-ica were junior colleges; the private two-year schools were far out-numbered by the public ones that enrolled primarily poorer students. Two-year enrollments increased over 33-fold, to nearly 150,000 students. At the conclusion of World War I, one out of every fifty undergraduates was enrolled in a junior college. On the eve of World War II, the proportion had jumped to one in six (Levine, 1986, pp. 162–177).

As public institutions multiplied, the character of the junior col-lege shifted away from the lower-division liberal arts curriculum. Vocational programs expanded. By 1930, there were more than 106 occupational curricula (Brint and Karabel, 1989, p. 180). Enroll-ments in these programs increased from one out of every one hun-dred students to one in ten (pp. 62–66).

Fewer students transferred. In 1919 more than two out of three went on to four-year schools; by 1930 that number was less than one out of three (Levine, D., 1986, p. 181).

As a group, the students attending junior colleges grew poorer as the number of public institutions increased. As early as 1929, a study showed that in California—the state with the most extensive public junior college system in the country—the proportion of lower-income students in two-year schools was more than three times greater than at four-year colleges (p. 181).

All of these trends became even more pronounced following the Second World War. The Truman Commission proposed a new role for the junior college. It suggested that two-year colleges become "community" colleges:

[T]his purpose requires . . . a variety of functions and programs. It will provide college education for the youth of
the community certainly, so as to remove geographic and
economic barriers to educational opportunity and dis-
cover and develop individual talents at low cost and
[with] easy access. But in addition, the community college will serve as an active center of adult education. It
will attempt to meet the total post–high school needs of
its community [President's Commission on Higher Education, 1947, pp. 67–68].

It was a radical vision of the junior college. And in the five
decades following World War II, it became a reality. As the president's commission had recommended, the number of institutions
expanded greatly. The 650 two-year schools in existence at the time
of the commission's report increased to nearly 1,500 by 1990. The
growth occurred almost entirely in the public sector. The 250 public junior colleges in existence at the time of Pearl Harbor increased
well over fourfold by 1991. In contrast, the number of private colleges shrunk from 317 to 167 over the same period, thereby consti-
tuting less than 15 percent of all community colleges (Cohen and
Brawer, 1982, p. 10).

Enrollments skyrocketed. They rose from half a million at the
time of the Truman Commission to 4.8 million in 1987 (Harris,
1972, p. 288; U.S. Census Bureau, 1990, p. 153). As the commission had proposed, occupational education became the focus of the
community college; terminal programs became the norm. By 1990
the rate of transfer to four-year institutions was 15 percent or less.
Currently, some experts say the transfer rate is as low as 5 percent
(Cohen and Brawer, 1982, p. 349; Brint and Karabel, 1989,
p. 153).

The student body mirrored the changes; the very affluent private college student disappeared. Sociologists Steven Brint and
Jerome Karabel described the change this way:

> The junior colleges had been predominantly middle-class institutions [before the war], but after the war they became predominantly lower middle-class and working-class institutions. Though estimates vary, it appears that students from lower-middle- and working-class backgrounds made up a majority, perhaps as much as two-thirds of the entrants of the public junior college in the first ten years after the war [Brint and Karabel, 1989, p. 94].

These trends have continued and grown. Today, the public community college enrolls a higher proportion of minorities (23 percent) than do four-year colleges (16 percent) (National Center for Education Statistics, 1989, pp. 170–171). It enrolls a student body whose parents have a lower level of schooling than any other sector of higher education: a majority of all undergraduates whose parents have less than a high school diploma attend a two-year school (p. 172). And it enrolls a population poorer than that attending any other sector of higher education. Today, 53 percent of all college students with family incomes under $14,000 (below the poverty line for a family of four) attend community colleges (pp. 171, 172).

If there can be said to be a home for the poor in higher education today, the once-elite junior college has become that place. By being the first institution to enroll each new disadvantaged population seeking to attend college, the community college performs what authors Steven Brint and Jerome Karabel call the "shock absorber" function in higher education.

Conclusion

In one fashion or another, America's colleges and universities have been open to the poor for more than three and a half centuries. For the most part, that openness has been passive: as a rule, it has been the responsibility of the poor to seek out higher education, not the other way around. The reverse has been true only in demographically or financially troubled times, when colleges tend to be more aggressive in recruiting students of all types.

Since at least the early nineteenth century, the openness of higher education has been differential, with poor students being more welcome at some institutions than at others. Over the last century and a half, the United States has developed three distinct sectors of higher education: an elite group of institutions composed of research universities and highly selective liberal arts colleges; a mass sector made up of moderately selective to less selective public and private colleges and universities; and an open-access sector incorporating community colleges and nonselective four-year schools.

In theory, a poor student can attend any college or university in America. Institutions have long boasted of their accessibility, but de facto stratification by income has existed for well over 200 years. The portals are far wider at the least wealthy, most marginal, and least selective institutions in the country; the number of poor students and the openness of the institutions to the poor are by far greatest in the third sector. To put it succinctly, the odds of a poor student attending a community college are considerably higher than the odds of the same student enrolling in an Ivy League university or other highly selective college. This is hardly news. However, what is of great concern is that the odds are even higher that a poor person, even one who graduates from high school, will not attend college at all. And in recent years the odds against the poor have grown increasingly larger.

II

Beating the Odds

3

A Portrait of
Twenty-Four
Who Succeeded

Part One leaves us with a simple question: What can be done to improve the odds that poor people face?

There are two very different ways of thinking about this question. The first and more desirable is to focus on pathologies or problems—that is, to ask what conditions keep poor people poor and bar them from the historic paths to social and economic mobility. Having identified the causes, the aim is to eliminate them.

Three times in this century, America has embraced this approach—during the Progressive era at the turn of the century, the Depression of the 1930s, and in the Great Society during the 1960s. Each period produced an outpouring of philanthropic concern and support, as evidenced by a flood of scholarly, artistic, and popular-media accounts of the plight of the poor. Social experiments designed to improve the lot of impoverished Americans multiplied. An army of advocates, experts, and social reformers claimed the national spotlight. And a deluge of social legislation from the federal and state governments on housing, jobs, income, and education followed.

In each instance, the nation's activism was short-lived. Concern with the condition of the poor waned; other social priorities captured the country's energies. In each case, the period was brought to a close by war—World War I, World War II, and Vietnam.

Each movement also brought with it a counterrevolution. In war's aftermath came a national sense of frustration with poverty—even an anger toward poor people. The problems of the poor seemed too large and intractable for the country to solve. Many of the social programs created were thought to be ineffective or, worse yet, misguided—costing too much and producing too little. Improvident Americans came to believe that they were being asked to do too much for the poor, while the poor were not doing enough for themselves. The biblical injunction that the poor would always be with us was accepted.

As a nation, we seem to be moving in this direction today. The difficulties of the middle class have come to overshadow the problems of the poor. The country is, sadly, less interested in trying to understand and eliminate the conditions that keep poor people in poverty.

This brings us to the second approach to improving the odds. It focuses not on the problems but on the solutions. Here, the emphasis is not on the majority of poor people mired in poverty but rather on the minority who manage to escape it. This approach emphasizes the anomalies. It asks what has worked in the lives of the people who somehow beat the odds and accepts the problems that poor people face as givens or black boxes. It plays down the role of these givens and instead seeks to identify how individuals manage to overcome them. The aim is to understand what makes it possible for some poor people to escape poverty and to apply that knowledge to help others do the same.

This approach is far more pragmatic than the first. Its greatest weakness is that it ignores root causes and accepts poverty as a continuing reality. Another limitation is that it is less ambitious, focusing on individuals rather than using a mass-market approach that emphasizes group or class. Yet the pragmatism of the approach brings with it some strengths. First, it is direct and very focused. It simply asks what works. Second, it has the potential to be implemented readily and quickly. It is a personal approach that focuses on individuals rather than on concerted changes in social policy. Third, it is, unfortunately, consistent with the times, in which social programs targeted at the poor are being dismantled by government.

The authors chose the second approach in an attempt to answer the question that began this chapter—what can be done to improve the odds facing the poor?

A Study

We looked at a particular group of success stories, the small percentage of the poor—people like Vest Monroe—who somehow make it to college. We specifically asked the "what" question intrinsic to the second approach: What happened in the lives of these people that enabled them to beat the odds? How did they come to attend college when their parents had not, when their neighbors had not, and when most students at their local schools had not? The aim of the study is to try to understand the reason for their success. Which factors—relationships, resources, and activities—made a difference? Is it possible to reproduce these factors and thereby enhance college opportunity and access for other poor people?

We focused on poor, first-generation college students. We interviewed a very small number of them—twenty-four—but their stories were so similar and so powerful that we decided to tell them.

We interviewed students attending two very different types of colleges—one an open-admission two-year college, the other one of the most selective universities in the United States. The schools were chosen to represent the greatest extremes in higher education available in this country. Beyond simply asking which factors made it possible for students to attend these colleges, we wanted to know whether there were different paths to different types of institutions of higher education for the poor. Are the factors that make it possible for a poor person to attend a low-cost, nonselective community college the same as those leading to an expensive, high-status university?

We also asked another question: are there differences among poor people with regard to the factors that encourage or enable them to attend college? Do age, gender, race, or birthplace make a difference? For example, are the stories of older or younger students the same? What about people of different races or from different parts of the country?

For the purposes of this study, each college initially identified twenty students who were poor (receiving full financial aid) and whose parents had not gone on to higher education, for a total of forty students. Also for purposes of the study, the students, as requested, varied by age, gender, race or ethnicity, and place of birth. All but six of the identified students agreed to participate in the study; two of the six could not be reached, and the rest declined to be interviewed. Of the remaining thirty-four, ten more were eliminated because they failed to meet the study's criteria—they were not poor, or their parents had attended college. Ultimately, twenty-four students met the criteria for the study and agreed to participate.

We interviewed each of the students. Our conversations were open-ended, lasting between an hour and a half and eight hours. Only one interview was less than two hours, and one took as long as eight. Several involved follow-up meetings. The focus was on how each student decided to attend college, what barriers and encouragements the student encountered, and why he or she chose a particular college. We guided each student through the story of his or her life, including discussion of family, friends, neighborhoods, schools, teachers, counselors, religion, out-of-school activities, aspirations, cultural events, educational choices and decision making, the comforts and discomforts of attending college, and the impact of college on current and previous relationships.

The people interviewed gave intimate accounts of their lives. In exchange, they were promised anonymity. In the pages that follow, their names are changed, and some particularly distinctive elements of their stories are masked. The colleges they attended are not named. Short biographies of the twenty-four people interviewed can be found in Appendix A.

Twenty-four Success Stories

The twenty-four people interviewed for this book have beaten very long odds. Though all were poor, none had succumbed to the war-zone environment in which most had lived their lives, nor had any settled for the temporary refuge of a bunker. They had constructed escape routes. They were not blocked by the obstacles that have made higher education historically inaccessible to the poor. Every one of these people found his or her way to college. Half (twelve) made their way to the highly selective research university—considered to be the peak of American higher education and the institution least hospitable to the poor. The rest (twelve) entered the sector of higher education most open to the poor, the community college.

The first reaction we had to this group was how different the individuals were from one another. They varied in age from eighteen to thirty-nine and were equally divided by gender (twelve men and twelve women). They came from every region of the United States—the West (six), the Midwest (two), the South (one), the Middle Atlantic states (two), and New England (nine); and around the globe, including the Caribbean (one), Asia (one), Europe (one), and the Middle East (one). They came from urban and rural areas. Racially, they were Caucasian (twelve), African American (four), Hispanic (five), Asian (two), and interracial (one).

Their families had dramatically different attitudes toward education. Some were sharply negative about school. For instance, Jenny, an eighteen-year-old North Dakotan attending the selective university, had fundamentalist parents who suggested that she leave school at age sixteen and get married. Billy, a twenty-seven-year-old community college student from Lawrence, Massachusetts, was told by his grandmother, "Don't waste your time going to school." His mother concurred, at least passively. She didn't go to PTA meetings. She didn't look at his homework. She didn't care about his report cards. And when he told her that he had decided to drop out of school, "she said, 'Fine.'" In Billy's house, "education was never pushed."

For others, education was the center of their universe, as it was for Lin, a twenty-year-old junior at the selective university. She came to the United States from Vietnam at the age of four and grew up in Detroit. For her parents, who operated a financially troubled inner-city grocery store, "school was like the important thing," according to Lin. Her parents talked about it incessantly. "It was like all sacrifices [should be] made for my sister and me to go to a good school and graduate from a good college and get a good job."

The school records of the twenty-four students varied just as widely. Academically, several of the students had performed very poorly. Dawn, a twenty-nine-year-old community college student from Rhode Island, had repeated the second and sixth grades, skipped many classes, "gave up" on school, and dropped out of tenth grade at the age of seventeen, when her first daughter was born. Others were at the top of their classes. Maria, a nineteen-year-old Floridian at the selective university, had always done well. She had maintained high grades, been in honors classes, won awards in statewide academic competitions, and attended a collegiate summer program during high school.

The types of schools the twenty-four students had attended were vastly different from one another. Some students—six of the twelve selective-university students, in fact—had attended prep schools or enriched, academically accelerated public high schools. These schools had enriched programs, strong faculties, superb physical plants, excellent guidance staffs, and they expected that all students would go on to college.

Other students had attended low-quality schools in poor neighborhoods. The story told by Sarah, now a junior at the selective university, is interesting because she saw both worlds. She had attended a public middle school in the South Bronx, where she grew up. The school building was badly run down. In recent years, there had been several cases of arson. More than half the students typically failed to graduate, and their scores on national reading tests were among the worst in the state. Faculty turnover was high; teacher commitment to the students and the school were low. Facilities and resources were inadequate; textbooks were too old and too few. Gangs dominated the school. Drugs were openly available, and weapons were common. In retrospect, Sarah said that it was an "awful" place. Sarah would see the other world when she attended a very competitive high school. The difference was dramatic.

The students interviewed had polar relationships with their teachers and school counselors. Billy grew up in a poor family, in a poor neighborhood and had attended—until he dropped out—poor schools. Billy remembered best a teacher who treated him like "a freak," called him by insulting nicknames, and humiliated him in front of the class. The experiences of Debbie, a twenty-nine-year-old divorced mother of two from Rhode Island, were more neutral. There were no influential teachers in her life. "I didn't even know my guidance counselor. . . . They didn't even know who you were." And Brenda, a twenty-one-year-old from a Chicago housing project who was now attending the selective university, had as good an experience in school as one could imagine. She lived with the family of her high school debate teacher after her divorced parents turned their backs on her.

Friendships differed just as markedly. Some of the students had many friends; others none. Sarah was one of those people who had no friends. She said that she "never really felt any connection with" her peers. "I was trying to please adults, and in the process [I] alienated myself from kids my age." In contrast, James, a nineteen-year-old Californian at the selective university, said he was "popular" and had lots of friends, but the relationships were never close.

Even among those who had friends, the relationships were widely different. Anita, a twenty-year-old from Boston at the selective university, had a few close friends, the college-bound kids she had studied and played with. "I would read a lot, hang out with my close friends, go swimming. My mother and me would go to the beach with my friends. My friends all loved my mother." For Billy, friendships were darker and destructive. "There was one guy who was a year ahead of me who was a friend of mine. . . . We cut classes. . . . The summer after elementary school, just prior to going to high school, I started drinking and [doing] drugs for recreation with friends. . . . I got drunk as a skunk. After that it became frequent." Billy and a friend broke into a home and stole a television set. Most of his friends never completed high school, and his mother had barred them from her home. Today a few are dead, and some are in prison.

The students also differed sharply in their beliefs and values. For example, religion was the touchstone in the lives of some; for others, it was irrelevant. For James, an evangelical Christian who prayed with his family for rent money and food, it was "very important. [The] guiding feature in [my] life is to know God." He viewed his education as an essential part of the Lord's plan for his life. But for Lester, an eighteen-year-old from Maine in his freshman year at the selective university, religion was not even a consideration. "The main motivational factor was myself. . . . I just wanted to show the world what I could do." When we talked about the place of religion in his life, he dismissed it, describing himself as a nonreligious person, a "Christmas-and-Easter Christian."

Damon, a nineteen-year-old from Harlem attending the selective university, described his church as a safety zone of sorts. But Damon didn't socialize with the church kids; even in elementary school, he had been more likely to play with the kids on his block. Being accepted in the neighborhood was more important to Damon than the church was. He saw no way in which the church had helped him leave Harlem or overcome his poverty. He said that telling congregations "the meek shall inherit the earth" and that they could enter the Kingdom of God probably kept some older people going. It gave them something to look forward to, but it did not do much for him. Nonetheless, Damon liked having the church nearby. He described it as "peaceful," "safe," and "good."

The one thing the students had in common was their poverty. Each had been a long shot to get into college, yet somehow all twenty-four of them had made it.

A Common Story

It is difficult to imagine a more heterogeneous group of people. But when asked how they came to attend college, each of them told almost the same story. It was remarkably like reading too many books by the same B novelist. The plot line, with few variations, was constant. The protagonists faced common challenges and overcame them in roughly the same fashion. The supporting players were almost interchangeable.

The story, put simply, was of an individual who touched or changed the students' lives. What mattered most was not carefully constructed educational policy but rather the intervention by one person at a critical point in the life of each student. Sometimes the mentor was a loving relative; other times it was someone paid to offer expert advice. In either case, it was the human contact that made the difference.

Interestingly, not one person attributed his or her decision to attend college to a program the student attended, despite the increase in early-intervention efforts in recent years. With one exception, Debbie, no one cited direct mail or mass media as a major influence, even though college marketing budgets have grown significantly larger and more sophisticated over the past two decades. Debbie talked about an individual who had been pushing her to attend college. One day a brochure arrived in the mail. She took it as a sign that the person was right, and she enrolled. As a rule, however, the students attributed the decision to go to college to an individual.

For Juan, an eighteen-year old from San Antonio attending the selective university, the influential person was his uncle. Juan was born in Mexico to parents with less than an elementary school education. When he was ten years old, Juan and his father entered the United States illegally to find work. They stayed with an uncle who, without asking permission, simply enrolled Juan in school; there was no choice in the matter. After two years, Juan and his father returned to Mexico, where Juan worked full-time in construction until the nation's poor economy brought him back to the United States. Once again, the uncle put him in school and convinced Juan, who was then fourteen, that his whole future depended on education. Juan stayed in school.

Nordim, a twenty-six-year-old Cambodian boat person enrolled at the community college, talked of an aunt who had immigrated to the United States before him. When he arrived in this country, after having experienced the horrors of the Pol Pot regime, forced relocations, refugee camps, and loss of most of his family, his aunt had already arranged English classes for Nordim, signed him up to take the GED test, and later arranged for him to enroll at the local community college she had attended.

For Lester, who was from a rural farm community, it was his sister who influenced him. Despite their parents' opposition to college, she made sure her brother would attend a nationally recognized university. She had rebelled against her parents earlier by enrolling in college, but she wanted better for her sibling. She learned about the intricacies of financial aid and convinced her brother that he could do it. He did.

The person who stood out in Damon's life was his father. Although Damon had lived in Harlem, he had attended an affluent prep school on Manhattan's posh Upper East Side. His mother died when he was a child. But, said Damon, his father "got the attitude that he wanted his kids to do better" than he had. He told his four children, "Study—the only thing that matters is your education." In thinking about how he got to college, Damon concluded, "I didn't have a whole lot of choice." His father had made it compulsory.

Fred, a twenty-three-year-old community college student from the Massachusetts South Shore, pointed to his mother, who had never finished secondary school but wished desperately that she had gone further in her education. When Fred dropped out of high school at the age of seventeen, his mother nagged him. She "pushed" him into the GED exam, according to Fred. Within two years of dropping out, she "forced" him to enroll at a local college. Fred wanted to make her proud.

Juanita's teachers were her biggest influence. At sixteen, after her unmarried mother had a heart attack, Juanita told her guidance counselor that she wanted to drop out of high school. Two years later Juanita was valedictorian of her southern Texas high school's graduating class, and she received a full scholarship to college. Her teachers had made the difference, she said. "I did really well in classes, so my teachers would try to drag me into things. . . . All of the teachers worked together. When the college process [began], they would . . . tell the counselors that 'she's really good. Help her out. Convince her to go to college . . . really far away.'" Her teachers arranged for Juanita to attend a summer program at an excellent out-of-state liberal arts college. They discouraged distractions. When Juanita began dating someone they considered the wrong kind of boy, a counselor and a teacher "called him out of his classes and said, 'you better be nice to her,'" she said. And finally, one of her teachers helped Juanita choose a college. "We sat there with Baron's Guide to College and just sort of went through all of them. She took a day off from school, and I took a day off from school. We . . . picked a college."

Lori also spoke of an influential person at school. A twenty-year-old now attending the community college, Lori had lived with her mother and two siblings in Massachusetts. The mother-daughter relationship was stormy. Lori was counseled for depression and had a poor school record because of truancy. After graduating from a vocational high school, she took a job in a salon as a cosmetologist. Two years later, finding the work was boring, Lori wanted a way out. She called her former high school guidance counselor and asked whether college was still a possibility. He said, "Absolutely," and told her how to go about it.

For Chris, a twenty-year-old from New Mexico, help came from a high school coach. Now a junior at the selective university, Chris had been academically strong in high school. His track coach told Chris—the first in his family to attend college—not to settle. The coach made him apply to the selective university rather than choosing the local public four-year school or a community college.

Dawn credited her attendance at college to the staff at the public housing project where she lived when she applied to college. Dawn, who had grown up in an alcoholic family broken by divorce, entered foster care at the age of eleven. The thirteen children in her family were sent to different homes in groups of two or three. After dropping out of school and having a baby, Dawn got married and had a second child. With her husband out of work, Dawn worked two or three jobs simultaneously in low-level service positions. The marriage was troubled, and Dawn decided to leave her husband, taking the two children with her. She was homeless for five months. After several unsatisfactory housing placements by social service agencies, Dawn and the children were given an apartment in a low-income housing project. She entered therapy and was directed to a GED program. The counseling staff at the housing department encouraged her to attend college. She tried it.

The person who made a difference in Barry's life was a vocational counselor. Barry had dropped out of a Providence, Rhode Island, high school in 1969. He had worked as a mover until injuring his back on the job at the age of thirty-five. Vocational counseling was part of the insurance settlement; through it, Barry learned he would never work as a mover again. His counselor took him through a vocational aptitude inventory, suggested hotel and restaurant management (which appealed to Barry), and identified a college that would provide him with the training he needed. Barry became a community college student.

For Meredith, a thirty-nine-year-old community college student from New Haven, Connecticut, a therapist made the difference. Meredith had grown up in a college town, dropped out of school, and spent the next two decades as an alcohol and heroin abuser. Her story is one of petty crimes, arrests, suicide attempts, periodic overdoses, frequent violence, and significant memory lapses. One night after shooting up, Meredith was unable to breathe. She thought she was going to die. This was not a new experience for her. What was new was a feeling—not of being afraid to die but rather of desiring to live. Meredith had thought that no hope was left. Treatment, therapy, and counseling followed. The therapist, who was also a recovering alcoholic, convinced Meredith that college was a possibility and made the contacts necessary to get her started.

And Leo, a twenty-two-year-old from the Canary Islands, gave credit to his next-door neighbor. New to the Northeast, Leo—who is wheelchair-bound and almost totally unable to speak due to polio—got acquainted with his neighbor, an adult college student. The neighbor told Leo that there were people just as handicapped as he was at the community college. Leo, who communicates by using a laptop computer, asked the neighbor how to apply. He enrolled the following term.

All but two of the people interviewed told a story like these— of the special person or people in their lives to whom they attributed their decision to go to college. What was remarkable was how much alike the two exceptions were. They were highly independent people who had no friends to speak of, no influential teachers or school counselors, and little family support. For all intents and purposes, they were self-contained people. Once they decided to attend college, they went ahead and did what was necessary to get there. Neither was able to pin down where the idea of attending college came from. Jenny, for instance, said that she had not really talked to anyone at school about college. She had been schooled at home by her parents until tenth grade, when she complained to the state that the education was not sufficiently rigorous. The state ordered that Jenny attend a regular high school. Up to that point Jenny's education had been highly independent, relying largely on books from the public library. She had no friends outside her parents and ten siblings, who all lived a hand-to-mouth existence at a religious retreat center. Jenny had learned about higher education and college admission policies by reading books and guides. She claimed that by the time she applied to college, she knew more about the topic than her teachers or guidance staff did. In fact, she had explained fee waivers to her counselor.

The other exception was Francois, a thirty-nine-year-old from the Dominican Republic. He grew up in a large extended family with two siblings. Neither of his parents had had much education. His father died when he was twelve, and Francois attended a Jesuit school until the age of thirteen, when he was expelled for being disrespectful. Thereafter, he attended public schools. Following graduation from high school, he came to the United States to join his mother, who had immigrated several years earlier. A series of jobs followed, including an occasional college course. Francois had always enjoyed reading, and the idea of taking classes just appealed to him. Francois, who is now divorced with twin three-year-old sons, said he decided to enroll in community college for the sake of his children. He felt he owed them the status of having a college-educated father. Francois had simply looked into local opportunities in higher education and enrolled. No one had assisted him in the decision.

So, with the exception of Jenny and Francois, all the students named a special person or persons to whom they attributed the decision to attend college. They named people as shown in Table 3.1.

What stood out was both how similar and how different these influential people were. They could not have varied more in terms of their places in the students' lives. They ranged from intimate family members to distant relatives, from school employees and neighbors to professional counselors. They were people who lived with the students from birth, or individuals who entered their lives only briefly in adulthood. It is difficult to imagine two more different types of people than Lin's parents and Barry's vocational counselor. Lin's parents were with her on two continents from the time she was born until she left for college. In contrast, Barry's counselor had entered his life after his thirty-fifth birthday. Barry estimated that, in total, they had spent much less than three hours talking about college.

What came through clearly in the interviews was that the timing—when the influential person entered the student's life—was at

Table 3.1. Influential Individuals Cited by the Students Interviewed.

Cited as influential	Number
Mother	3
Father	2
Both parents	1
Other family members	4
Neighbor	1
Teacher	2
Coach	1
Guidance counselor	1
Vocational counselor	1
Human-services officer	3
Therapist	3
None	2

least as important as who the influential person was. The contact had to be made when the student was ready for it; Barry said that his teachers had recommended college to him before he dropped out of high school, but he had felt that they did not know what they were talking about. Meredith reported that her parents had attempted the same, but she blew them off. Debbie had acquaintances who had gone on to college and encouraged her to go. However, neither the advice nor the acquaintances had impressed her. Dawn grew up believing that college was not for people like her; no one could convince her otherwise when she was a teenager. In a similar vein, Damon said that if his father had not been there to push him to college during his childhood, he had no doubt he would have ended up like the other kids on the block—using drugs, dropping out, and being unemployed.

It is remarkable that most of the interviewees had not chosen the special people in their lives; in general, the special people had identified *them*. Put another way, it was quite unusual that a potential student would explicitly seek out someone to guide him or her to college. There were exceptions. Lela, a twenty-nine-year-old

Iranian refugee attending the community college, was determined to find out how she might enroll in higher education and deliberately sought guidance. Similarly, when Lori decided she wanted to go to college, she sought out the one person she knew who might be able to advise her about whether it was possible. In the other cases, it was the influential person who first suggested the idea of college. The students may have initiated contact with the influential person, particularly when the individual was in a helping profession; however, the explicit purpose of learning about college had not been the reason for getting together.

For some of the students, the suggestion that they could go to college came as a surprise. Barry, for instance, said he never thought of college as being the answer to his physical disability and his inability to return to his old job. We asked him why not. After all, college was not a new idea to him. It had been proposed earlier in his life. He shrugged, saying he had rejected it long ago as not for him and didn't think of it again. But when the vocational counselor suggested it, Barry thought college sounded like the right thing to do. It was that simple.

Ironically, the people who identified the students and had such a large influence on them differed enormously in how much they knew about higher education. At one extreme was a counselor of Brenda's at an elite private girls' school. The counselor had attended an Ivy League college, earned a graduate degree, visited an assortment of colleges each year, had contacts in admissions offices around the country, and could speak knowledgeably about the differences between similar kinds of schools. At the other extreme was Maria's mother, a Colombian immigrant to the United States who had never finished primary school and knew little about college. But she was a passionate believer in education who wanted a better life for her daughter. Maria's mother had never heard of Brown University, one of the schools where Maria was admitted. Nor did she have any idea where Rhode Island was on a U.S. map. She was shocked to find that it was near Canada. However, the night before she was to have major cancer surgery, Maria's mother made her daughter promise that she would attend one of the Ivy League universities that had accepted her—despite mounting pressure from aunts, uncles, and grandparents in Colombia to stay near her ill parent.

Maria's mother made up for her deficiencies in knowledge about college by cultivating teachers. She was always talking to them. "She sent them gifts for being helpful," said Maria. "My mom would make them enchiladas and rice for dinner. They'd come over. . . . My mom would call them up."

Juan's uncle was a lot like Maria's mom. He did not know much about education and had not gone very far in school. He had failed to complete primary school, but he did not try to overcome his limitations. Instead, he played to his strengths, hooking Juan on school during his nephew's elementary and junior high school years. By the time Juan had surpassed his uncle educationally, he was college bound and capable of fending for himself.

Another difference among the people who encouraged the interviewees to attend college is that they used very different methods to influence the students. Some were principally talkers. They were people like Lin's parents and Fred's mother who knew little about education but a lot about Lin and Fred. They spoke from the heart, lovingly extolling the value of college and its centrality to a good life. For them, higher education was an article of faith. Lin said that it was "like a religion to my father"; Lin's parents and Fred's mother gave sermons. College was more a moral issue to them than a rational or practical decision. At the other extreme were Leo's neighbor and Barry's counselors. These were people who knew a lot about college and relatively little about the people they introduced to higher education. They passed on what amounted to expert knowledge—the who, how, what, when, where, and why of college. They spoke from the point of view of people who knew the facts. Their conversations were far shorter in duration, less emotional in content, and much more pragmatic than Lin's or Fred's parents.

Other influential people went beyond talk. They were activists—people like Juanita's teachers, Nordim's aunt, Lester's sister, and Meredith's therapist. They made appointments, arranged contacts, and even chose colleges. Nordim said his aunt was so busy making arrangements that she never stopped to explain anything. Juanita's teachers represented the extreme. They had developed enrichment experiences intended to enhance Juanita's chances of getting into a "good" college, and they worked to eliminate the potential pitfalls, such as boyfriends from the wrong side of the tracks. The activists left nothing to chance. Their goal was not counseling but ensuring that the student ended up in college—and often in a particular type of institution.

Despite the differences in who these people were, how much they knew about college, how much time they spent with the students, when they entered the students' lives, and which methods they used to help the students, they all accomplished pretty much the same goals.

We asked the students what made these people in their lives so special. What did they do for the students? What did they get out of the relationships?

The answers fell into four somewhat overlapping categories. One response was that the influential people imparted hope—they gave the students a sense of greater possibilities than they had imagined, and instilled in them a belief that those possibilities might be achievable.

Damon described it this way:

> Kids in my . . . neighborhood have to deal with so much violence and anger that they feel trapped. They feel like they don't have a lot of opportunity. . . . The job market for the most part is flipping burgers. . . The kids on the block never talked about college. They talked about making money, making the dollar, getting over until next time. . . . They wanted to leave the city, . . . but they had no sort of place other than selling drugs.

Damon recognized early that he was different from the other kids on his block. He said his father gave him a dream:

> I started to realize we did sort of see things different. I had some of these goals that were maybe imposed by my parents . . . I sort of had this idea that I'm working to achieve something later. . . . I knew I had to work and keep achieving.

Barry was deeply depressed after he had hurt his back and was forced to give up not only his job but life as he knew it. Barry loved working as a mover, meeting people, being independent, and traveling all over the country. With the accident, his world seemed to collapse around him. He said that his counselor's suggestion of college gave him a new lifeline. It gave him some hope about tomorrow, which he had not had for a long time.

After her divorce and homelessness, Dawn and her two children were placed by social services in a motel off an interstate highway. The family lived in one room and had no car. The motel was inaccessible by public transportation. Dawn said that it was like being in prison. Homelessness in some ways seemed preferable, she said, except in inclement weather. She had never felt so low in her entire life. When she was finally moved to public housing, Dawn was physically comfortable—even elated—but she still had no idea what to do with her life. When a housing-project staffer counseled her to go to college, she was overcome emotionally. All her life she had assumed that college was not for people like her. For the first time, Dawn said, she had "hope" and "a real dream." It seemed "too good to be true."

Perhaps Juan put it best. From the time he was a kid, he thought his whole life would be in manual labor or low-paying service jobs. His uncle, and later his principal, opened his eyes to a new world he never knew about or even imagined. "It was amazing," Juan said.

The special people in the lives of the interviewees were responsible for enlarging their vision, offering dreams of a better tomorrow not found in their neighborhoods, and making those dreams seem attainable.

A second outcome of the students' special relationships was enhanced confidence. A therapist assured Peggy—a thirty-one-year-old divorced mother of two who had not been in school for more than a decade—that she had the aptitude to complete college. Leo's neighbor told him that handicapped people were succeeding in higher education. And Sarah's parents told her, "You can go wherever you want to college." The influential people gave the students a sense of confidence and convinced them that they could achieve the dream.

Billy's confidence hit rock-bottom following a general discharge from the navy after several episodes of being absent without leave. Billy had believed that he was "worthless" and "good for nothing." He said, "There were many times that I thought I was smart enough and thought that I could benefit from college, [but] it was an impossibility." When a therapist suggested college and told him he could succeed there, Billy reluctantly gave it a try.

Chris said, "My coach told me I could do it," and Chris believed him. Lori said that her guidance counselor really encouraged her to go to college. She "took his word for it." Similarly, Meredith explained her decision to enroll in college by saying, "This is where my therapist told me to go." James said his parents always told him that "you can be whatever you want." He wanted to be president of the United States; they never told him to choose something more reasonable or more practical. They simply told him he needed a good education to prepare for the job, and that he had the ability to go to a good school. The influential people built the interviewees' confidence and gave them the courage to take a risk.

The third contribution students mentioned was that the special people stressed the importance of education. They persuaded the students that the only path to life success or to achieving their dreams was schooling; the two were inextricably interlocked. This theme came up repeatedly in the interviews. Sometimes it was stated negatively. As Juan put it:

> I knew if I started work [instead of completing school and attending college], I would end up like some people I know . . . who didn't go to school and when [they were] thirty years old were washing dishes.

More often it was said positively, like Lin's comment:

> I want an education, and I want to have a really good career. The only way to do this is to go to college.

Juanita made the same point even more concretely. When she told her guidance counselor that she was dropping out of high school to assist her family, the counselor said simply, "Don't—you will be able to do much more for them with an education."

Fred said that after he dropped out his mother told him again and again, "If you don't go to school, you'll end up like I did. You don't want to do that. School is the key to your future." The notion of school as a key to the future was almost a mantra to Maria and Lin: their parents let them know this every day by word or deed, whether it was the dreaded education lecture by Lin's father or the long daily discussion of what was going on in school at Maria's house. The students in this study placed a high value on education, and they said that the special people in their lives were responsible for teaching them that lesson, or driving it home.

Finally, the students cited the influential people for placing them at the college gate. Whether figuratively or literally, these people put the student and the college together. That's what Juan's uncle, Nordim's aunt, Lester's sister, Damon's father, Fred's mother, Juanita's teacher, Lori's guidance counselor, Chris's coach, Dawn's housing staff, Barry's counselor, Meredith's therapist, Leo's neighbor, and all the others did.

What comes through clearly in this study is that the most valuable mechanism for steering students from poverty to college is people. Human contact is what makes the difference.

All kinds of names are given to the process by which this occurs. "Mentoring" is the term currently in vogue. The recent popularity of the word has devalued its original meaning. It has come to stand for little more than a tutoring relationship—one person assisting another. The role of the special people in the interviewee's lives, however, is something more akin to the historical root of the word.

Mentor was a character in Homer's epic *The Odyssey*. On leaving for the Trojan Wars, Odysseus, Lord of Ithaca, asked his close friend Mentor to take charge of his household and to care for his son Telemachus. Odysseus was gone for twenty years. In his absence, a group of 108 suitors—the leading young men of Ithaca—laid siege to his home; attempted to court his loyal wife, Penelope; and plundered his wealth. The goddess Athene, daughter of Zeus, assumed the shape of Mentor. She encouraged Telemachus to search for his father, obtained for him a speedy ship and an excellent crew, and accompanied him on the voyage, serving as captain. When Telemachus returned home with Odysseus, Athene (again in the guise of Mentor) gave him the courage—despite his fears and doubts—to slay the suitors. She protected Telemachus from their spears, led him into battle, and when the bloodshed was done established peace between Odysseus and the friends and relatives of the suitors, his Ithaca countrymen.

The historic Mentor was a person who spoke with the voice of the gods. He instilled hope, built confidence, knew what was important, and offered direction. On a less godlike scale, this is precisely what the people in the lives of the students in our study did. They were mentors in the original—and best—sense of the word.

These modern-day mentors performed their work in very different ways. The next two chapters examine these variations in the context of the two most divergent groups in this book: young people who went to an elite university immediately after high school, and older adults who went to a community college following a hiatus from schooling. No two groups varied more in terms of who intervened in their lives, when they intervened, and how long the interventions lasted.

4

. . . .

Hitting the Jackpot
Entree to the Elites

T welve of the students interviewed attend the selective university. Reflecting national statistics, they are younger than their peers in community college. They are of traditional college age: the youngest is eighteen and the oldest twenty-one. The university students are also more geographically dispersed. Whereas the two-year college students tend to live near the school, the selective university students come from all over the country—the West (five), the Midwest (two), the Middle Atlantic states (two), New England (two), and the South (one). The university students are more racially diverse than the community college students as well, contradicting national statistics. They are Hispanic (five), Caucasian (three), African American (two), Asian (one), and interracial (one).

What the selective university students have in common as a group, however, is that they have beaten the longest odds. Not only did they avoid succumbing to the environment in which they had grown up, but they enrolled in the sector of higher education that was traditionally least accessible to the poor. These are the students who somehow managed to hit the jackpot.

The irony is that they accomplished this with a surprising level of ease. As a group, the students attracted mentors early in their lives, and the mentors worked with them over extended periods of time. As a result, applying to and being accepted at a selective university seemed almost a natural occurrence—destiny rather than a freak event or an accident.

When asked how they came to attend college, all but one of the university students attributed the decision to at least one significant person in their lives. (The exception was Jenny, whose guidance counselor, as we said earlier, didn't even know her name.) The special people shared one distinctive characteristic: every one of them came from a primary institution in the lives of children—families and schools. All of the university students named either relatives or teachers; family members were named three times as frequently as teachers. Not one university student cited a therapist, rehabilitation counselor, or human services officer (See Table 4.1).

The consequence was that the university students had mentors with relatively little experience in higher education—far less than the special people cited by the community college students. Only one-third of the mentors had attended college themselves. The compensation for lack of knowledge about higher education was time. The mentors of the university students intervened in their lives for much longer periods than did the mentors of community college students. With two exceptions, the latest that any mentor's intervention began among university students was during middle school, and once begun, the intervention continued through college admission. The exceptions were Jenny, who had no mentor, and Chris, for whom the special person was a high school coach.

This pattern—particularly the lack of expertise about higher education by the mentors—was at first surprising. But it is actually quite logical and should have been anticipated, as the university students' mentors came from primary institutions. By definition, family members were people who had not attended college; and parents and teachers typically spend more time with their children (and begin spending that time with them earlier) than do the more expert individuals this book credits with being mentors—external surrogates, such as therapists and rehabilitation counselors. Interestingly, the university students built such strong emotional relationships with their mentors, even when they were not family

Table 4.1. Influential Individuals Cited by the Selective University Students.

Cited as influential	Number
Mother	2
Father	2
Both parents	1
Other family members	3
Teacher	2
Coach	1
None	1

members, that they often kept in touch with them throughout college. They sought their mentors' advice even when the mentors could no longer be considered experts. For instance, upon being admitted to several Ivy League medical schools, Juanita called her mentor, a high school teacher, for advice on which one to attend.

Also worth noting is that the university students had a greater number of special people in their lives than did the community college students. For example, in the cases of Anita and Juanita, it was a succession of teachers rather than a single individual who made the difference, although both chose one individual as being singularly important. Juanita's case was interesting. She had several teachers working on her behalf, sometimes simultaneously without each others' knowledge and sometimes collectively. In Anita's case, the teachers acted in succession, passing her one to the next as she advanced in grade level. Similarly for James and Lin, it was the whole family rather than a particular person who steered them to college. While James received encouragement and support from his parents and siblings alike, Lin had more specialized arrangements. Her parents served as general cheerleaders and critics, while her older sister showed her the ropes, providing practical guidance about what to do. But not all the university students had more than one special person in their lives. Lester, for instance, had only his sister—no teachers, no parents, no counselors, no friends—no one else.

The multiplicity of influential people in the lives of the university students had an important result: it meant that students were more likely to meet someone along the way who was sophisticated about colleges and college admissions, even if their principal mentor knew little about higher education. There was a tendency—again by no means universal—for students once discovered to be passed up a chain to more and more informed people. Juan was an example. His uncle, who knew nothing about college, enrolled him in primary school. Juan's middle school principal encouraged him to apply to a selective high school. A supportive teacher at the high school then sent Juan to a savvy guidance counselor, who got him to apply to a selective university.

Collaboration among the influential people in the students' lives was very common. Sometimes it was simply a confluence of plans. For example, Juan's uncle and his high school counselor pushed him in the same direction, though not through any joint effort. For several others, however, the collaboration was intentional. Anita was a prime example. Her mother encouraged her to go to college. Anita's friends were the very small coterie of college-bound students at her school. Anita's teachers thought she was special and were grooming her for college with a series of enrichment activities—honors classes, extra-credit projects, extracurricular activities, and summer programs. Anita's mother invited her daughter's friends to her home and took them places with Anita. She kept in touch with the friends' mothers, and she invited Anita's teachers to family events. They came. In addition, Anita's teachers were involved with Anita and her friends outside of school. They invited Anita to their homes, retained her as a baby-sitter, and participated together in service activities after school. When her mother died, Anita's aunt filled a similar role. Every significant person in Anita's life reinforced every other one. The effect was to turn a potential escape route into a virtual superhighway to a college education.

One result of all the attention bestowed on them was that the university students were surprisingly sophisticated about college issues. For example, when asked how they had gotten up the nerve to apply to a school that costs more than their families made last year, not one student was fazed by the question; most even shrugged it off. Each talked about financial aid; several mentioned fee waivers. A third of the students had their campus visits paid for by civic or alumni groups. There was little mystery about college, and little hand-wringing about how they could afford it; they understood what they were talking about. Only James, who knew a great deal about college finances, gave even a remotely different answer. He said that his future was in the hands of God. He had prayed for financial aid and for wisdom in deciding which school to attend.

The students also thought they were special. Anita said she lived a "charmed life." Her observation was probably not so far off the mark. The reality is that for a poor person, being admitted to a highly selective university was not a matter of luck, of being in the right place at the right time. It was not something that occurred out of the blue, like the young woman who was discovered sitting on a stool at Schwab's drugstore and went on to become a movie star.

For the poor people profiled in this book, the process of being discovered began with early identification. During a conversation with one of the university students, an interviewer asked, "When did you know you were special?" The interviewer was not even sure that the student knew what he meant by the question. However, without missing a beat, the student answered, "In the third grade," with the same certainty and confidence he had when he told the interviewer how many siblings he had. The question had made sense to him. In fact, only one of the university students—Jenny— was perplexed by the interview question. Ironically, Jenny was also the only university student planning to drop out. It is also impor- tant to note that she was the only university student without a men- tor. All the rest had known by junior high school that they were special or different from their peers, and many had known as early as elementary school. James said, "I was always special and unique, and people always flocked to me." In contrast, the sense of being special was rare among the community college students; only two responded affirmatively to the question.

The sense of specialness came in many ways, through good grades, honors classes, and awards. As Lin put it, reflecting the experience of most of the other university students, "I would always win awards like history fair, valedictorian, national merit." When she had arrived in the United States, Lin did not speak English. "After I overcame the language barrier, which took about a year and a half—two years. Since I was little, . . . I don't mean to brag, but I always did, like, get top grades." The sense of specialness also came from kind words and being treated differently. Anita's experience was typical:

> There were six of us that my second-grade teacher [called] "the dynamic six." We were the only people who cared about school work or cared enough to get A's and B's instead of C's and D's. . . . Most of my teachers would have to give me extra work or stuff to do, because I would finish work faster. My third-grade teacher used to complain that I read too much. . . . In grade school . . . they would give buttons for honor roll. I got them. There were various certificates. . . . There wasn't really a valedictorian in grade school, but I was selected to be valedictorian.

Once, Anita got into a fight with another student. The principal didn't ask who started it; she simply disciplined the other student. Anita was told again and again throughout her childhood that she was different and that she was special. She believed it.

When the university students were asked when they had made the decision to apply to college, they always answered that it was in late high school. When asked whether they had done anything special to prepare for college, the answer was generally no. When asked to think about their answer a bit longer, or when questioned about specific activities in which they might have engaged, the students cited a torrent of activities that had preceded their decision. Damon, from an inner-city black neighborhood, was an example. He answered no to the initial query, but after the follow-up he said, "Wait, did I tell you about," (indicating that it was almost an after-thought) "attending a summer program at Cambridge University in England?" Like him, a number of the Cambridge attendees were minorities. During the summer program, the students were ad-dressed by outstanding educators. As a result, Damon met one of his heroes, a black activist-educator, during that visit. Prior to Cam-bridge, Damon had been involved in an academically enriched sum-mer camp, a selective preparatory school, interschool academic competitions, and more.

With the exception of Jenny, every student interviewed at the selective university had a similar background. Extensive enrichment activities were common in each of their lives. They had attended summer schools and taken SAT preparation courses. They had engaged in—and won awards in—interschool academic competi-tions, sometimes at the state level. There were science fairs and olympiads, academic decathlons, debate societies, and much more. Three students—Lin, Juanita, and Damon—had attended college programs during high school. Others—including Maria, Damon, Chris, Sarah, and Juan—had had opportunities to travel abroad. Seven of the twelve who attended academically enriched schools had special opportunities as part of their daily curriculum.

The intriguing fact is that the students did not usually choose these activities for themselves; they were generally guided into them by the special people in their lives. Juanita, for example, had always done well in school. In her words, her teachers had "pushed" her into activities. They got her involved in an academic decathlon, a math club, an SAT preparation course, the state sci-ence fair, the choir, a dance club, and a course on ecology at the local university. Finally, one teacher got Juanita a grant to go to one of the nation's more prestigious liberal arts colleges for a sum-mer program in creative writing and computer languages. The

teacher convinced Juanita and her mother, despite their strong initial opposition, that the summer program in the midwest was
important. When Juanita returned from college at the end of the
summer, she wanted to attend a first-rate university outside of
Texas.

The students who had attended summer college programs at
places such as Stanford, Cambridge, and Oberlin had similar experiences. In every case, they had loved the summer. The students
they had met, many of whom came from similar backgrounds, were
more stimulating than any group they had encountered previously.
The courses they took were intellectually richer than the classes
they had attended in school, and the teachers were top-notch. In
each instance, the students had decided as a result of the summer
experience to attend an out-of-town, selective university.

For the students at the selective university, the cumulative effect
of the enrichment activities was a gradual and continuing change
in their life trajectories. An escape route—not merely out of the
war zone of poverty but well into the middle class—was being fash-
ioned. The process was so gradual and so well crafted that most of
the students were not even aware it was happening, as evidenced
by their initial lack of comprehension regarding the import of activities in which they had participated in preparation for the selective
university.

The opposite side of the coin is that the students also avoided
the pitfalls that might have derailed them from their collegiate
course. Their sense of specialness seemed to ward off the destructive behaviors of their peers, such as substance abuse and even early
pregnancy. For some, it was a matter of personal choice. For example, James avoided the neighborhood kids, who were on a very different path from his, by spending time with his parents and
siblings.

> I did things with my family. I didn't really have close friends in
> high school. Looking back on it, I didn't because my family
> was my best friends.

In contrast, Lester had rejected his parents. His father "hated" his applying to a selective university. He wanted Lester to stay home, to "not lose track of home life" and the "people in the community." Lester cut his ties with his father and turned to his sister, who encouraged him. After enrolling in the selective university, he even stopped coming home.

For Damon, the choice was school over the neighborhood kids and the war zone. He spent twelve hours a day away from home in classes, extracurricular activities, and commuting to school. On top of that, there was homework. For Damon, "it was really hard to associate with anyone else because of the time left."

Others were simply very selective in choosing friends. They sought out people like themselves. Chris said he did not associate with kids from families like his. "I didn't have much interest in that. We didn't have the same values, like school. They were more interested in getting drunk on Friday nights. I wasn't."

Maria expressed the same sentiments. She lived in a Catholic, first-generation Hispanic neighborhood in which Spanish was the primary language and none of the people there went to college. She had only two or three "really, really close friends," she said, "the ones who went on to college" from high school. "We [had] that in common." She didn't play with the neighborhood kids.

Another reason that many of the students had stayed on the track to their elite university was that they were frequently rejected by those living in their neighborhoods. For instance, Damon not only lacked time for the other children in his neighborhood, they also turned away from him. They saw him as different and by the start of junior high school had told him:

> You talk proper. You went to a school downtown. . . . He's
> uppity. I'm not going to hang around with him. So I really
> didn't hang around with too many people after that.

Sarah told a similar story. She said that her schoolmates in the South Bronx were mostly "Spanish."

Because that's where the neighborhood was. There were a couple of other white girls. By the time we got to eighth grade there were only five boys left. . . . Basically, I wasn't very popular with the remaining girls.

Brenda had been rejected by her family. Her mother had left home; her stepfather had remarried, refused to pay for Brenda's schooling, and lost interest in her. It was fine with him when Brenda went to live with her grandmother and subsequently the family of one of her teachers.

Whether it came as a matter of rejection or personal choice, the students at the selective university exhibited a remarkable degree of isolation in childhood and high school. Anita, for instance, said she had lived in a "bubble." Peer relationships were a good example. As many as half of the students made statements such as these:

"I didn't have any friends."

"No friends."

"I didn't really have close friends."

"I felt quite isolated."

"Solitary."

"I never felt any connection with [my peers]."

Among the other half of the university students, friendship circles were highly restrictive. The female students tended to have had a very few (two or three) close college-bound friends with whom they did everything. Lin was a good example. She had three close friends, but during the summer she would visit with them primarily in the afternoon; mornings were reserved for SAT preparation. The male students were more likely to have had a range of acquaintances but few if any close friends. Juan, for instance, said he knew a lot of people in the neighborhood but hadn't done anything with them socially. He would talk with them in his uncle's grocery store, where he worked when he was not in school or doing homework. He had no close friends at school, either.

What came through regularly, almost uniformly, in conversations with the students was a sense of aloneness and separateness. This should not be confused with loneliness, which was very rare. Although several of the students—especially Sarah—questioned whether the isolation was desirable, only one student, Jenny, said she was currently lonely. Rather, the students had a feeling of independence and self-reliance, which seemed very much a part of their sense of specialness. In some ways, this became a cocoon of sorts, insulating the students to protect them from the onslaught of the neighborhood.

In this respect, the most powerful cocoon that the students encountered was the preparatory school. Over half of the university students had attended such schools—public and private, sectarian and nonsectarian. James, Anita, and Juan had attended selective Catholic schools; Brenda and Damon had been enrolled in elite private day schools. And Sarah and Lin had attended very competitive public schools requiring admission tests. The rest of the university students had gone to local public schools. Again, Jenny was the exception: most of her schooling had occurred at home, although she had spent one year at a religious academy and another in public school.

The effect of the prep school on poor kids was to intensify the focus on college, with a premium, or special emphasis, placed on highly selective schools. For example, Sarah said that upon graduating from the Bronx High School of Science, "the natural follow-up, the thing you do afterward, is usually [to] go on to college. . . . The ultimate is an Ivy League school." This certainly was not true of her neighborhood or the school she would have attended there. She said that the children in her neighborhood—with whom she did not associate—were interested in smoking, drugs, and drinking.

Sarah said she was "not a prude" but was more interested in school. Her three close high school friends also attended Bronx Science and lived outside her neighborhood.

At the same time, because all or nearly all of the prep school students were college bound, the impact was to intensify peer group support. Brenda described the atmosphere at her private girls' school this way:

> Ninety-nine point nine-nine percent of everybody [goes] to college. There's a bulletin board—the senior Daisy Board. The daisy was the school logo. In the center of each daisy is the name of a college and each petal was a student who decided to go to school there. . . . Everybody went to college. The only person who didn't go to college [didn't go] because she had been hospitalized for anorexia. She went . . . second semester.

In addition, the prep schools provided more knowledgeable adult support from guidance counselors and teachers on matters such as financial aid, testing, and deadlines. Also, representatives of highly selective universities visited the prep schools annually. James said that he had been barraged with announcements about college at his private preparatory school. Every day there were announcements over the public-address system about which colleges were visiting, dates for exams, scholarships for different groups, and the like. They were impossible to miss, and they provided James with his principal education about college, even though he did not graduate from this school.

Enrichment activities were also more numerous and more easily accessible at prep schools. Brenda told of talking to a guidance counselor about her lack of plans for the summer before her junior year of prep school. The counselor suggested applying to Andover or Exeter in New England and helped Brenda make the arrangements. Damon's school sent him to Cambridge, England, and Sarah's school took her on a trip to the Soviet Union. These were the sorts of opportunities that were not available to students at the neighborhood schools.

Therefore, prep schools had the effect of turning what people in the poor neighborhood saw as aberrant behavior—going to college—into a norm and an expectation for the poor students. In prep school, the students were going with the tide, not against it.

In each case, the prep school also physically removed the students from their neighborhood and took them out of the war zone. However, this was not without cost to poor students in terms of self-esteem and social fit. Although nearly all of them had made friends—sometimes like them, sometimes different—in college, most of the students interviewed (83 percent) had experienced a sense of discontinuity between their backgrounds and the elite schools they attended at some point in their academic careers.

Brenda and Damon, the two students from the wealthier private academies who had both grown up in poor black neighborhoods, experienced the discontinuity at their prep schools. Brenda described the experience this way:

> [The] social elite sent their daughters to [my] school. . . . They had all these youth groups . . . the same churches and church trips. I wasn't ever part of that. It was hurtful and hard to understand. . . . I never thought of myself in socioeconomic terms.

For both Brenda and Damon, the transition to a selective university was easy. Brenda found the differences between herself and other students less daunting than those she had encountered at the prep school. Damon, too, said that he had seen it all before at prep school; coming to the university was an improvement. There were many more blacks at his college than in his prep school.

For the other students, however, the discontinuity struck hardest in college. This was true even for Sarah and Lin. Although they had attended academically enriched public schools, their fellow students there had been principally from the working class, in contrast to the much more affluent students they encountered at the selective university. Juanita told the story of a cousin who came to visit her at the university. "He was vocal and loud [like the people at home]. A lot of my roommates didn't understand and thought he was rude and obnoxious. It was like both worlds colliding." It reminded Juanita how different she was from the others at the college. She could not wait for her cousin to leave.

Juan expressed similar feelings in different words. He said, "I feel like everybody here knows everybody else, but no one knows me." Others pointed to specific differences between themselves and the more traditional selective university students.

"I didn't get their jokes."

"I wore the wrong clothes."

"Their music was weird."

"I hated the food."

"I didn't know which utensils to use [when eating]."

Poor students regularly felt a sense of being in limbo in their elite education. Not only did they feel that they were different from other university students, they also fit less well in the world from which they came. Chris put it this way:

I am so different than anyone in my extended family, even now, my immediate family. When I go back, they look at me differently. It's very subtle. I don't mean this in a derogatory manner, but they're just a little bit ignorant, naive about a lot of things. They're mainly concerned with getting by because that's all they have. Everyone in the family is basically blue-collar . . . they're operating forklifts, working at Stop and Go, like a 7–11 or a Store 24. . . . The pay that comes with those jobs isn't great. . . . My goals are very different from theirs.

The same feelings were expressed again and again in the interviews.

> "When I go home . . . we never talk about school. They don't understand much about it."

> "I rarely talked to my parents about . . . my going to college."

> "I've been trying to keep these things glossed over."

> "My personality at school is very different from my personality at home."

> "I go back and it usually takes me a week. Things are a little bizarre. . . . You go back and feel uncomfortable."

> "I've been feeling really guilty, 'cause I never really thought [about] the effect of my going to school and not helping [my family] out financially."

> "[W]e don't really connect."

> "Initial reaction to college—resentment by relatives."

In many respects, poor students at the university were "hyphenated" people, torn between two cultures, fitting comfortably into neither. Juan said that there was no one at home he could talk to about college, so he didn't speak about it when he was home. Maria said that her mother is very happy for her but has no idea what her life is like—she can't understand it but wants desperately to be a part of it. College has pulled them apart. She laughed and said that it was even worse with her relatives in Colombia. Her grandmother, badly misinterpreting Maria's college life, believes she went to school in Asia. The students interviewed have been left hanging between two worlds—between their past and their present—not totally a part of either. Yet, increasingly, the students have tended to think of the selective university as home, rather than the places from which they came.

In this sense, the university students have paid a price for their success. Many outgrew the mentors—usually intimate family members—who had done so much to shape their lives. There were exceptions. Brenda said that she remains close to her debate coach, who came from a background similar to hers. Juanita is still in regular touch with her teacher, who plans to attend her graduation from the selective university. Lester and Lin remain very close to their sisters, who are college graduates.

In summary, the students who attended the selective university shared many characteristics. First, their attendance was not an accident or a last-minute happening; the construction of an escape route from poverty to a university education began early in life. Second, the primary institutions worked for these students—the mentors in their lives came from their families and schools. Third, the students needed only one special person to help them construct an escape route, but most had more than one; often, several worked collaboratively. Fourth, the preparatory school proved to be a very powerful vehicle for getting poor children to college. Fifth, the process of moving poor students toward the selective university usually involved a gradual shift in their trajectory, as opposed to a drastic or sudden change.

The students did not fit well with the families or neighborhoods from which they came, nor with the colleges they were currently attending. The fit with the colleges was better than that with their homes, however. The situation of poor adult students attending a community college is very different. The interventions did not come as early in their lives; the primary institutions let them down; and the escape routes took longer to construct and were more treacherous.

5

. . . .

Betting the Farm

The Struggle to Get in the Door

The twelve adult community college students were split evenly by gender. Their ages ranged from twenty to thirty-nine; both the median and mode were twenty-nine. For the most part, they had grown up in cities and towns near their college. Two-thirds came from southern New England, while the others had been born abroad and resettled in southern New England. Reflecting the demographics of the region, most of the students were Caucasian (nine); the remaining students were African American (two) or Asian (one).

No group of people in this study had a more difficult time getting to college than adults who had grown up poor. In sharp contrast to the students at the selective university, the primary institutions—families and schools, and all the other institutions prominent in children's lives—churches, neighbors, friends—had failed the community college students.

Billy's family is an example. Billy was born in Lawrence, Massachusetts—ranked as the twenty-third–poorest city in the United States. His father, whom he described as "an extremely miserable persecuted guy" was an alcoholic who started Billy drinking by giving him cups of beer in grade school. His older brother, whom Billy regarded as a role model, started drinking and using drugs early and is now in prison for bank robbery. Physical abuse was a regular part of growing up for Billy, and friends were never allowed to visit his home. Bad things were expected; successes were ignored. For instance, if Billy received a high test score in school, his parents were uninterested. In contrast, poor grades got "So what did you expect?" looks. His parents only wanted Billy to leave them alone. His friends came from similar backgrounds—many worse.

Growing up, Billy did not think that his family or neighborhood was in any way abnormal; he didn't know that anything else was possible. Billy thought that everyone lived in a world like his, or worse.

> What is amazing when you think about it, some people think
> when they're growing up in a really bad environment, . . .
> that's the way it is everywhere . . . all my friends as far as I was
> concerned were worse off than I.

Debbie's story was also representative. Like most of the two-year college students, Debbie had endured a deeply troubled family life. Her parents, neither of whom had completed secondary school, divorced when she was nine. Her father never paid child support. In fact, he left the family suddenly, sold all their possessions (including the children's toys), and pocketed the proceeds for himself. As a result, life afterward "was tough." The family was forced onto the welfare rolls. They moved in with Debbie's grandmother, sleeping on couches and sharing beds, and Debbie's mother took a full-time job at night. As the oldest in the family, Debbie assumed the role of mother to her three siblings. She was angry, and communication between mother and daughter deteriorated badly. Debbie avoided her mother as much as possible. When Debbie turned fourteen, her mother told her to get a job.

School was another problem area for Debbie. It had never been her mother's biggest priority. After the divorce, Debbie's grades got progressively lower; no one said anything about the decline. If Debbie had access to a guidance counselor, she was unaware of it, and the only teacher who had showed any interest in her life had left the school. Debbie spent as little time as possible at school—only two hours a day in her junior and senior years of high school. She skipped the courses needed for college.

Friends did not provide support. In fact, they were not an important part of Debbie's life. The family moved so often that long-term friendships could not be sustained. Debbie was always the new kid, the outsider.

Church was a "negative" experience for her, too. Debbie put it this way:

> I had a bad experience there. . . . As a child, I went every Sunday. . . As a teenager, my eyes started opening up to what was going on around me. People were doing this to that one, gossiping. . . . There were bad things happening. This was not what church is supposed to be for.

We asked Debbie whether anybody had taken a special interest in her when she was growing up. Her answer was a quick and definitive "no."

Most of the adults in this book had experiences similar to Debbie's. With regard to their families, three-quarters of the community college students had grown up with either one parent or no parents at home. While this had also been true for half of the students at the selective university, the community college students' families were more dysfunctional: almost half had reported alcoholic parents, and a third talked of physical abuse at home.

School was comparable to their home lives. In contrast to the students at the selective university, who were academically high achievers, half of the two-year college students had dropped out of high school. A majority (seven of the twelve) had poor school records, academically or socially. In general, this was not true of the students who had immigrated to the United States. With the exception of Francois, who had been expelled from school for his conduct, the immigrant students did well academically. Their schooling had simply been interrupted by conditions in their home countries or their families.

Generally, the primary institutions that the community college students had encountered in childhood either functioned as war zones or were at best bunkers. They did not provide escape routes, at least not via education.

This was reflected in the life histories of the community college students. Prior to attending college, half were participants in social-welfare programs; economically, two-thirds would be classified as poor and the remainder working-class.

Only Barry had a long and stable job history. Many of the students—including Dawn, Billy, Fred, Debbie, Meredith, Francois, and Lela—had had a succession of positions intermixed with periods of unemployment or parenthood. The jobs the students held were blue-collar or service positions ranging from soldier, truck driver, and assembly-line worker to cosmetologist, sandwich maker, and convenience-store cashier. Debbie is something of an exception; she had been in training for an advanced technical position in the military before her children were born.

Romantic relationships had not gone particularly well for the community college students either. Only one student was married at the time of the interviews; five others were divorced. The rest were single. Among those who had never been married, several complained about having a history of troubled relationships. In all, the divorced students and the never-married students in troubled relationships together accounted for 75 percent of the two-year college students interviewed.

Nonetheless, prior to making the decision to attend college, each of the students had established a life for himself or herself that did not include college, or for that matter necessitate higher education. It had taken an epiphany or a dramatic life change to bring the adults interviewed for this book to a campus. Marital breakups were often a precipitating factor for women. This was true for three of the students—Peggy, Debbie, and Dawn—who together represented half of the community college women interviewed. Each had come to higher education following a divorce, and each attributed her readiness to attend college to the breakup. Peggy's story is a familiar one.

> I was in North Carolina and my husband had moved out. . . . Things had gone bad. . . . I was thinking to myself, 'I'll be on welfare. Chances of me getting a job are going to be slim and none because there are no jobs available.'

> I was very depressed. . . . I called my mother and said, 'I have a lot to ask you and I don't know how to ask you.' She already knew. I moved from a three-bedroom wonderful home to an attic room with two kids [in her mother's home]. I sold everything. . . . I was on welfare. For the first seven or eight months . . . I slept at least nineteen hours day. I'd get up, get the kids to school, go back to bed, wake up, go get them, fix them something, go back to sleep, wake up, put them to bed, go back to sleep. I was depressed.

> I decided I had to go do something about it. I thought about college, but at the time my mind was frazzled. I didn't know what to do. Someone told me about the [local community college]. It's very accessible. I got right off the train into school.

The disorientation and depression following divorce, as well as the need for education, were common themes in the accounts of the divorced women interviewed.

Immigration was another life change that led to college. Lela's experience was typical in several respects. Born in Armenia, she was adopted by an Iranian couple—a sixty-year-old man and his thirty-five-year-old second wife. The wife had favored the adoption for monetary reasons, believing that a judicious early marriage to a successful son-in-law would bring the family financial security. When Lela was in fifth grade, her adoptive mother told her that it was time to quit school. "You better marry someone. I don't want you any-more." But Lela—who wanted an education—persisted, with sup-port from her father. However, when he grew sickly and finally died, Lela was forced to leave school, abandon her dream of college, and marry as her mother had wished. Then came the Islamic revolution. As a Christian in Iran, Lela had an even more difficult life. With her husband, her two children, her mother, and her mother's sister, Lela fled the country, finding political asylum in Germany; it was as far as the family could afford to go. After saving for two years, they were able to resettle in the United States, and Lela resumed her education.

All of the adult students who had emigrated to America—Lela, Nordim, Leo, and Francois—told similar stories of an education interrupted by conditions in their homelands or families and of opportunity made possible by a move to the United States.

Illness was a third motivating force for attending college. Barry's back injury, Meredith's drug abuse, and Billy's alcoholism had ultimately led each to enroll in higher education following rehabilitation.

With two exceptions—Lori and Fred—all of the adults inter-viewed had experienced a precipitating event of one sort or another before enrolling in college (see Table 5.1). Lori, a twenty-year-old, was the youngest community college student interviewed. In con-trast to the older adults already well into their lives, Lori was young and unmarried, lived with her parents, and still had contact with her guidance counselor. These factors made it much easier for her to make the transition from beautician's salon to college. Fred's story was similar. He too was young (twenty-three), lived with his mother, had not been out of high school very long, and was being pressured by his family to resume his education.

In contrast to students who went on to college right after high school or soon thereafter, the move to college by older adults was traumatic. It was not the gradual change in trajectory experienced by the students at the selective university. It represented a profound

Table 5.1. Precipitating Events.

Precipitating Event	Number
Immigration	4
Divorce	3
Illness or injury	3
None	2

and disruptive life shift for most of the older adults, no matter how much time had gone into thinking about it. This is probably why it had taken a dramatic event for them to change directions.

Like the younger, selective university students, eleven of the adults had special or influential people in their lives to whom they attributed their decision to attend college. It's notable—and consistent with the nature of the change that college represented for the adults—that the majority of the influential people came from secondary or safety-net institutions, including therapists, counselors, and others from the helping professions. They filled in for the primary institutions that had failed the community college students (see Table 5.2).

While all of the selective university students who had mentors found them either in the family or the school, this was true for only three of the community college students; two were the younger students, Lori and Fred, who lived with their families and were only recently out of high school. Fred cited his mother, and Lori selected her guidance counselor, as special people in their lives. The third exception was an immigrant, Nordim, who credited his aunt. As a group, the immigrants were more inclined to attend college than were the other adults; the fact that they had not done so prior to coming to the United States was largely a matter of circumstances in their home countries rather than problems with health, substance abuse, or self-esteem. The only other student with a mentor not from either the helping professions or the primary institutions of family and school was also an immigrant: Leo chose his neighbor.

Table 5.2. Influential Individuals Cited by the Community College Students.

Cited as influential	Number
Human-services officer	3
Therapist	3
Mother	1
Other family members	1
Neighbor	1
Vocational counselor	1
Guidance counselor	1
None	1

In general, the adults had spent relatively little time with the special people who had counseled them into attending college. Therapeutic relationships tended to be the most sustained. Otherwise, the students' contact with special people could be measured in weeks or days. Besides the two students—Nordim and Fred—who had selected relatives as mentors, the community college student who had spent the most time with a special person prior to enrolling in college was Billy; he had been seeing his therapist for a little over a year.

The job of these influential people was different for the adults in community colleges than for the younger university students. The adults needed all the things the younger students did—a dream, the means for achieving that dream, and self-confidence. But the adults were ready, and they wanted both a chance and a change, at the time the influential person entered their lives. What they most needed was direction, information, and reassurance. Billy described his state of mind when his counselor talked to him about college. "Occasionally I would meet somebody who would say I was bright. For a time I would be motivated, then I would say I know they won't take me. I guess I just got tired of coming to that point." Billy wanted to be convinced he could succeed at college if he chose to. His counselor had done that for him.

The shaping or enrichment experiences of the younger university students were absent for the adults. So, too, was the history of successes the young people had enjoyed, as well as their relative sophistication about higher education. One of the younger adult students, Fred, differed somewhat. He was identified in school as a precocious youngster and was accelerated in his early elementary school years, but he soon lost interest in education and fell behind his classmates.

In contrast to the younger students, the adults worried a great deal about their intellectual competence when they arrived at college. By the time Fred enrolled in college due to his mother's nagging, he had forgotten his early successes and had very real doubts about his ability. Debbie, who is bright and articulate, put it this way: "I was petrified. Here I am an older woman in her late twenties with two little kids." Throughout five years of marriage her ex-husband had told Debbie that she was stupid and "so uneducated" that they "couldn't have a conversation."

Lori grew up thinking the same way: "I remember always feeling like I was different from everyone, whether it was my voice or something inside me. . . . They didn't want to accept me." College seemed like a "stretch" for her. Billy, who was well spoken and intelligent, felt similarly. He said, "I've never finished anything. I think this is going to be really difficult. . . . For some people [like me], it's more difficult." This was true for Nordim as well. He said, "It was hard. It's still hard for me to describe. I didn't have a good feeling at all for at least a few months." Meredith, too, was very scared. She had not been around college people and didn't understand the things they thought were funny. She didn't even know the appropriate etiquette for cafeteria dining, which things were finger food and which were not. Intellectually, she felt entirely out of the league of her fellow students and the faculty. As she put it, "I had no confidence, and my self-esteem was nil."

Dawn also found herself to be at a real disadvantage. "For kids coming out of high school . . . it's a lot simpler for them. . . . I wish

I could do that. Maybe I'm always thinking about my kids, my family. That's why I have more things to deal with than they do." Failure had become a norm in school as well as in relationships for many of the older students, and their academic confidence was low.

As a result, getting a college degree meant more to the adults than it did to the younger students at the selective university; the younger students were more likely to view a degree as instrumental, a card to be punched on the way to a much larger dream. In contrast, most of the adults saw the degree as an end, a personal statement about their competence and achievements. Peggy, in her thirties, said:

> I'm going to be the first one to graduate in my family. I'm going to have a degree and that is going to mean something to me. It is only an associate degree, but it's mine and I earned it. That's more than some people can say. Not that I want to be better than them, but I've done something and I'm going to have some recognition.

Debbie expressed the same sentiments.

> Well, I figure a lot of dreams I had before never went through . . . nothing is going to stand in my way. I'm going to do it. Sometimes I get stressed and I just want to drop out of school. I'll go work in some store and make $5.50 an hour or something. No, I'm better than that. I can do something. . . . No one in my family has ever done it.

Meredith put it most simply. She measures her self-worth by her performance.

Correspondingly, the career aspirations of the adults were not as high as the younger students'. Young people have big dreams; this was particularly true of students at the selective university. Professional careers in business, law, and medicine were the most common aspirations. But many hoped to achieve even more: a couple of the students talked about becoming president of the United States, and one wanted to be "master of the universe."

By comparison, the adult students were more likely to choose careers in accounting, computing, nursing, office work, and human services. Debbie had shrugged off a professor who told her she should think about law school—she thought he was just being polite. Meredith said that she really wanted to go to medical school but thought it was impossible. When her college counselor said it was possible, Meredith questioned the counselor's judgment. Lela was the only real exception among the community college students. She said, "I do believe that whatever I want in my life, I can do it. Nothing can stop me."

Hand in hand with low career aspirations came a low level of knowledge about college. Money—and the lack thereof—was a constant theme in the adults' conversations. As Lela said, "I don't know how far I can go. Every minute I feel myself on a rope that might be cut off because [it's] being supported by government." The dollar amounts the students worried about were small. For example, a lack of money for car fare and books led Nordim's brother to quit college. The irony of the situation is that the selective university students did not worry about where they would find $25,000 a year for tuition and expenses, whereas the community college students would leave college for the lack of a few hundred dollars. For Fred, even the thought of attending a residential college was a "major fantasy"—something to dream about but never do. The community college was all he could ever really hope for.

One dramatic difference between the selective university and community college students was their understanding of financial aid. As Debbie explained, "Nobody ever said to me, 'You can have financial aid. There is some kind of assistance.' All I could think is. 'I can't pay somebody back. I cannot do this.' Being on welfare for so many years, I did not want to be in the system." When she first arrived at college, Debbie knew nothing about financial aid, so she scraped together the money to pay her tuition. She borrowed. She charged her credit card to the limit. Debbie only later learned about financial aid by accident while talking to another student. She considered herself lucky, since "a lot of students drop out."

In contrast to the students at the selective university, the adult students had a great deal of misinformation about financial aid. Billy, for instance, assumed that because he had moved in with his parents he did not qualify for financial aid. He wanted to go to college and thought he was bright enough to succeed, but he dismissed the prospect. "It was an impossibility because there's no money. If you don't have money you can't go to school. . . . I was just desperate." Similarly, Debbie believed she did not qualify for financial aid because she had lived out of state for several years, and Lela concluded that she could not get aid because she was born outside the United States.

Dawn was one of the few students who understood financial aid. A counselor at her housing project sent her to the higher-education information center at the local public library. There she was taken through the labyrinth of forms and taught about fee waivers.

Beyond the financial problems, going to college created difficulties for all the adults interviewed. One problem was a lack of support from spouses; not one of the women attending the community college had a husband or significant other who encouraged her. When Meredith told her live-in boyfriend she had decided to go to college, his response was, "You mean you're not going to work for two years? How are we going to live?" Francois was the only one who said his spouse was encouraging.

Friendships broke down, too. Prior to entering college, the adults interviewed did not for the most part have friends who were college educated. Dawn had met several college graduates at her housing project who told her to give it a try, but more commonly, going to college drove a wedge into the existing relationships of the community college students. Meredith talked about the end of one friendship. She compared going to college with "looking through the wrong end of a telescope. My world was getting bigger and bigger and [my friend's] was not changing. I couldn't deal with that. I stopped contact with her."

College also disrupted home life. Homework and classes took time away from children. The interviewees, particularly the women, expressed both guilt and resentment—guilt for how few hours they were able to spend with their children, and resentment for having to skimp on their schoolwork to be with their children. Debbie talked about the tensions between school and family. "I value education. I think it's important, but I also know that I have responsibilities. I do want to go on, but at this point I need to work and leave school. I have two children. I'm by myself, and my mother's ill." Francois was angry that school robbed him of the time he wanted to spend with his children. Nordim said that all he did was work to earn money, go to school, and sleep. Debbie highlighted the continued juggling between home and school. "I'm taking three years to get my two-year degree here because I do have the children, and I do have to be home when they're home. I rush out when they leave and I rush back to get home before them." Dawn had turned the juggling into a science.

> I get up early in the morning. My days usually start between six o'clock and seven. The first thing is to get everybody dressed and ready to go out the door. Now, since I've moved, I've had help with transporting Samantha to and from her day care. . . . A friend of mine does take Samantha to and from. The girls, I make sure they get ready, have their breakfast, and they're out the door. Basically, all are out of here by eight in the morning, and my first class starts at eight twenty-five. It's rush, rush. I can make it to the station, which is nearby. It's really convenient. Then, I try and do all my work, especially the computer work, in school, because I don't have the use of a computer at home. Whatever I don't finish I try and get done when I get home from school before my other two get home, and by the

time the baby gets home. Before I know it, it's dinner time, we eat. I save all my heavy cleaning for the weekends when I do have my time off. My daughters help out a lot . . . so everything works out.

Problems of this sort were far worse for the older students than for their younger counterparts at the university because college profoundly disrupted their daily lives. The adults were not immersed in the academic world in the way the younger students were; their lives were more interdependent and complicated. They had well-established lives with families, homes, friendships, and regular daily activities. The adults, with the exception of the youngest students, did not go to college with the expectation of making new friends or as a first step in leaving established relationships. Instead, upon enrolling in college they found that they no longer fit into the world in which they lived. While the world remained the same, they changed. For some, the college route took them further than they anticipated or ever wanted to go.

For many, relationships blossomed as a result of attending the community college, even though they had not expected this. There the students found people like themselves and began to associate with them, usually as acquaintances rather than close friends. Meredith pointed out that there were a number of recovering drug abusers at the community college. Billy said the same of alcoholics. Leo spoke of handicapped people. Lori noted the number of students of traditional college age. And Debbie and Peggy talked of the single mothers on campus.

One organization appeared to have the ability to ease the adults' transition from poverty to higher education, functioning as the equivalent of the preparatory school for younger people. It was the military. Two of the community college students had served in the armed forces. For Billy, the navy had provided a way out of the war zone, got him a high school diploma, and given him advanced training in radio. It could have given him even more, but alcohol and drug use—combined with frequent unexcused absences—had resulted in a medical discharge.

Debbie got far more out of the military experience. She joined right out of high school. The army had raised her job trajectory, placing Debbie in a training program in military intelligence. No one in her family had ever been in such a prestigious position. Debbie was influenced by the army's stress on education for positions such as hers. Debbie received two years of instruction in her field, with further education on the horizon and officer candidate school a distinct possibility for the future. The army had given Debbie confidence and increased her self-esteem—she had held a 99.38 percent average in her advanced training program. And finally, through international assignments, the military had shown Debbie a world very different from the war zone in which she had lived. After the birth of her children, Debbie retired from the military.

For the most part, poor kids grow up to be poor adults, and the cycle continues. Occasionally it breaks, however. One mechanism adults use to better their lives is attending a college, often a local community college.

Indeed, poor adults attending two-year colleges were unique in several respects. First, an epiphany or a dramatic life change had usually been required to bring them to a campus. Second, the primary institutions had generally failed to provide support for them. The special people in their lives came principally from secondary or safety-net institutions—therapists, counselors, and other service providers. Younger two-year students and immigrants to the United States were exceptions; the special people in their lives were usually relatives or representatives of primary institutions. For the younger students, this was because their lives were not as firmly established as those of older adults and because they were in closer proximity to their families or schools. For immigrants, it was because the life events that forced them off the college trajectory were aspects of life in their country of origin, not the United States.

Third, in contrast to the selective university students, there was typically only one special person in the lives of poor adults. The contact tended to be short-term, and the influential person operated principally by offering expert information.

Fourth, the prep school proved useful for the university students by providing an escape route. For community college students it was a different institution—the military—that proved quite useful in helping adults escape poverty.

Finally, compared with the students at the selective university, the poor adults at the community college were less sophisticated about college, had lower career aspirations, had achieved fewer successes in education, and had experienced greater disruption in their lives due to college. In short, for a poor adult, attending a community college proved to be more difficult and jarring than enrolling in a highly selective university at traditional college age.

III

$\cdot\ \cdot$

Improving the Odds

6

Nine Mentors
Who Changed the Odds

We conducted our interviews with the college students over a two-year period. As we spoke to more and more of the students and heard them describe their common journey, we found ourselves becoming increasingly interested, perhaps even fascinated is not an overstatement, by their mentors. We kept asking ourselves, What, if anything, do the mentors have in common? What does Maria's mother, living in poverty with less than an elementary school education, have in common with Billy's therapist—a psychiatrist and affluent woman who had attended college for more than a decade? How had such very different people come to play the same role? How in a sense had they become interchangeable? We decided to find out.

We interviewed nine of the mentors. There was nothing magical or even scientific about this number. By the time we decided to talk with the mentors, we had lost contact with several of the students. They had relocated, graduated, transferred, or left college. The community college students were particularly difficult to keep track of. In the end, we sought to meet as diverse a group of mentors as we could imagine. Three of the mentors were relatives of the students—a parent, a sibling, and an uncle. Another three worked in schools—one in a public school, one in a parochial school, and one in a highly selective preparatory school. And the last three mentors worked in safety-net or human-services professions—one as a psychiatrist, one as an officer in a housing project, and one as the head of a literacy agency.

The Relatives

We met Maria's mother, Helen Barrientos, in her home in a Miami barrio. The doors and windows of the house were covered with bars. Burglars had recently blown a hole in the back of the house and stolen the television and the few other items of value that Barrientos owned. Maria, home from school on break, served as translator—her mother speaks only a little English, and the interviewer spoke even less Spanish.

Barrientos, a petite woman in her fifties, cooked lunch for the visitors just as she had done for Maria's teachers in the past. Everything about Barrientos is quiet, well organized, and dignified: her speech, her appearance, her home. In preparation for this meeting, she had written an autobiographical sketch.

Barrientos had grown up in a small mining town in Colombia. Her family of nine was poor, and the untimely death of her father had made things even worse. However, Barrientos said that even though her parents had lacked money, they had given her strong values and a positive attitude. The little education she received was at home and came from her mother, an herbal "doctor" who helped the sick people of the community. Barrientos was fascinated by books and as a child had sneaked any book she could find into her bedroom to read under the covers at night. She also listened to the radio to learn about the world beyond her village; her favorite program was "Dr. I.Q." While still a teenager, she was forced to leave home to earn money for the family. She found a succession of jobs in laboratories and health facilities. Starting out doing the scut work, Barrientos rose to increasingly technical positions, drawing and testing blood samples. Ultimately she came to the United States illegally to find work.

Once in this country, Barrientos initially found work in a blood bank, then moved on to doing lab work for a doctor at a university and finally in a hospital lab in Miami. Along the way, she had an affair with a married doctor; the affair produced Maria. Barrientos quickly came to realize that in the United States one needed a diploma for almost any job. She was determined to give Maria a better life.

We met Juan's uncle, Carlos Gomez, in his restaurant in San Antonio. It is a family-style restaurant in a Latino community. The interview began before the restaurant had opened for breakfast. As Mrs. Gomez was preparing the day's food, we sat around a table and talked. As Mr. Gomez spoke, members of the family stopped by periodically—Mrs. Gomez, the couple's children, and their nephew Juan, who was home from the selective university and was serving as translator.

Gomez, an impassioned and very likeable man in his early forties, cooked a special meal for the group. He is muscular in appearance, voluble in speech, and didactic in style. There was much that he was eager to tell us. We talked of Juan's impending graduation in the following year—the entire extended family expected to attend.

Carlos Gomez grew up on a farm in Mexico. He always wanted to go to school, but it was never possible. His family was large and had no money, so Gomez had only a few interrupted years of formal education. As a young man he moved to Mexico City and got a job cleaning out bullfight arenas. There he met people who had been to college. He realized that he needed to learn how to dress, talk, and even eat differently to be accepted for higher-paying work. He wanted to learn many things, and because of his financial situation he knew he would have to do so through work rather than school.

He came to Texas because he thought he could earn more money in the United States. There he found a job making couches.

Gomez saw that "America had many laws" and that formal training was required for almost any good job or opportunity. He held a succession of menial positions, from delivering milk to packing meat. A man who worked with Gomez told him that he could be anything he wanted if he followed his dream.

He liked living in the United States because here he met more people who believed in education than had his acquaintances back in Mexico. Gomez saw how much better the college-educated people of the community lived. He found a friend from home who had become an engineer. He also saw friends from Mexico who had given up the future for liquor. He discouraged drinking among his friends and family members in his new life in Texas and instead stressed hard work and education.

Based on these experiences, Gomez took a big risk that changed his life. After marrying a Latina from Texas, he saved all the money he could and sold their few possessions to start a business. The couple thought that their best prospect would be a restaurant. They began with a hole-in-the-wall establishment and traded up to their current business, buying real estate along the way. The business became their whole life, and the future was for their children.

The Gomezes enrolled their children in Catholic school after having bad experiences with the public schools. They made frequent visits to talk with teachers about how the children were doing. The results were mixed. One son had gotten in with the wrong crowd, and a daughter had gotten pregnant and dropped out of school. Another son is going to the same selective high school that Juan had attended. The other two children are doing well.

With his faith in education, Gomez helped his nephew enter the selective Catholic school and eased his transition to the new environment. For example, the new school required taking frequent showers, a request that Juan found alien and frightening until his uncle helped him understand. Beyond this, there was not much Gomez could do for his nephew because of his limited education, but he had told Juan repeatedly, "If you are not taught to do something, you lose."

Lester's sister, Karen Gilman, asked us to meet her at her office in the suburbs of Washington, D.C. We talked over coffee in a restaurant in the same building. A single woman in her late twenties, Karen Gilman is professional in appearance and adventurous in spirit. She and Lester grew up on an isolated farm in rural Maine. Life was simple. Their parents had stressed the importance of hard work and doing well in school, although their father had only an eighth-grade education and their mother had done just a bit of nursing training. Their parents, now divorced, were "distant," and the family atmosphere was strained. With few other children around, Lester and Karen learned to like each other's company, despite the six years' difference in their ages.

Gilman's social activities were generally limited to school and church youth groups. School was strict and the punishments for bad behavior were severe, but Gilman kept her grades up to remain eligible for sports and to maintain her spot on the baton-twirling team. A number of the students in her school had considered going to college but had limited their ambitions to the local community college or nearby state university. The more attractive options for high school graduates, however, were returning to the family farm, getting married, or joining the army. Attending a local college was the expectation for both Karen and Lester. Ms. Gilman, however, wanted out of her small town; she hated it. Through baton-twirling and sports, she had seen life in other places. For her, college was the "stage coach the heck out of Dodge."

Gilman left her small town and attended college out of state, raising cocker spaniels to earn extra money. Her parents—particularly her father—were not happy when she moved East after graduation because she wanted to "live in a big city." After a stint in Seattle, she found a job at an investment firm outside of Washington, D.C.

Gilman had always known that Lester was special and told him so. She was not surprised when her brother's SAT scores "were through the roof." She encouraged him to apply to college out of state and told him not to worry about money or logistics or their parents. He "would find a way."

The Teachers

Brenda's debate coach, Margaret Wilson, picked up the interviewers at a Chicago hotel and drove to the very selective preparatory school where she works. It is a magnificent campus, with facilities that would make many college personnel drool. Its students, who dress in uniforms, come from the most prominent families in the area. Wilson, who is in her late forties, is enthusiastic, funny, and easy to talk with. She made us feel as if we had known her all our lives.

Mrs. Wilson was born in Houston and raised in Texas before she settled in Chicago as an adult. At one time, both of her parents had been missionaries. Her mother had one year of college behind her, and her father, a truck driver, had only an eighth-grade education. Yet it was her father who had inspired Wilson with his "faith in education." Her father had grown up during the Depression and always spoke of the value of "hard work" and "education." Wilson said that she had absorbed his values. School and especially church groups were very important to her. Most of Wilson's high school friends had aspired to college; they were not big-time troublemakers, and most did well in school. A teacher in Wilson's high school sparked her interest in debate (not to mention the presence of "a cute guy" on the team). Traveling with the debate team allowed Wilson to see other parts of the country.

Wilson's belief in education was carried into adult life and influenced her career choice. She became a teacher because she felt that teaching was compatible with marriage. The man she would ultimately marry, now a neurosurgeon, came from a similar background. They met at a church function; his parents had also been missionaries. They both believed in self-sacrifice to help others. Not too long after they were married, Wilson and her husband became foster parents to a sixteen-year-old girl who stayed with them for only a short time. Next, they provided a more permanent home for two children, a brother and sister, ages eight and ten. Those children became members of the Wilson family, along with the couple's two biological children. She and her husband "collected" needy kids. At various times they took in a Vietnamese girl and a Nigerian girl with medical needs, which were supervised by Wilson's husband. They also gave a home to Brenda.

Wilson loves teaching debate, particularly to young girls who need the confidence to speak out. She feels excited about and satisfied with her work. For recreation, she enjoys travel but especially loves playing the accordion in a polka band.

We visited with Lori's guidance counselor, David Goodman, in a very different setting from Wilson's. He works in a badly worn public high school that could not be easily confused with the campus where Margaret Wilson teaches: the students here are much more diverse and come from the opposite end of the economic spectrum. In contrast to Margaret Wilson's posh suburban community, Goodman's school is located in a dying working-class town.

Goodman talked to us in his office. In the anteroom, a dozen students were taking the equivalent of a time-out, a psychological break. While we spoke, the phone rang off the hook, and students and parents wandered in. Goodman had a brief conversation with a parent about how to prepare for juvenile court with her son. Goodman apologized profusely for the interruptions. He is a gregarious man who clearly loves his work and likes to tell visitors all about it. Although he is beyond traditional retirement age, he enjoys what he is doing too much to seriously consider leaving it. Goodman's office is cluttered, and we had a sense that his life is, too.

David Goodman's parents were Russian immigrants who spoke very little English. For Goodman, books were "magic," and his father, a grocery clerk, brought him books whenever possible. He lived in a large, extended Jewish family that stressed education. As a child during the Depression, Goodman was instilled with a strong work ethic, but he always felt that a career in teaching was more "secure" than one in business—less tenuous and risky. He served in the military during World War II, which helped give him a glimpse of the larger world. The G.I. Bill made it possible for him to go to a local college.

Goodman became a husband, a father, and a science teacher, and he enjoyed all three roles. Gradually, he became more interested in counseling students. He believes that his generation had clear goals and a strong sense of right and wrong but that too few students today have such solid guideposts. In 1972, three boys from his school were involved in a drug-related crime; someone was killed. He knew the boys and felt that a sympathetic ear and his training as a guidance counselor was not enough. Goodman completed a Ph.D. in psychology and became a special-needs expert, taking on the role of student advocate in the school system. He remained in the job despite periodic and considerable opposition from school administrators who were bothered by the constant collection of troubled kids in his anteroom. Goodman's office is a place where any student can come and talk—and they do. Like many other students at the school, Lori kept in touch with Goodman even after her high school graduation.

David Goodman claims that he is considering retirement and contemplating a move closer to the ocean, which he loves. Actually, he says, he's only pretending: talking about retirement makes his wife happy. She wants to go to Florida. For now, he fills his leisure hours as a part-time art dealer and by selling fish at a pet store he co-owns.

Our conversation with Bob Anderson, one of Anita's teachers, was the only interview that did not take place in person. After repeated attempts to get together failed, we decided to try talking over the phone. Anderson described himself as thirty-eight years of age, balding, and looking like someone who enjoys eating (which he does). He is pragmatic and introspective, and he has a sense of humor. He knows what it feels like to be an outsider.

We subsequently visited the high school where Anderson teaches. It is a Catholic school in one of the poorest areas of Boston. The school is selective, and the surrounding neighborhood is poor and Hispanic.

Anderson grew up as an only child in Boston. His mother had attended business school, but his father had no college education at all and had worked at a blue-collar job. When Bob Anderson was only ten, his father died, causing grave financial hardship for him and his mother. Anderson's grandparents, with whom he was very close, passed away soon after his father. Anderson's mother was an at-home mom who was always "class mother" when he was in elementary school. But after his father's death, she had to get a job outside the home. Bob felt alone and different, but his mother helped and encouraged him in his school work. He thought that this is what had pushed him into the teaching profession.

Growing up, Anderson neither smoked nor drank, and church was important to him. He was not an athlete; when the other kids played ball, he watched television. His group of friends were not in the "brain group," but he aspired to college anyway. He was a mediocre student in high school.

After a succession of teaching positions and a hiatus to see what life was like outside the world of education, Anderson started teaching at his current school and has remained here for more than twelve years. He loves his work and the kids in the school. He sometimes finds it hard to keep working at his low salary, but he loves "being in the trenches" and inspiring kids like Anita to achieve all they can. Anderson's other loves are bookstores and good restaurants, and he is also currently pursuing a master's degree in theology. He considers himself a loner. He is single and lives with his mother.

The Human-Services Professionals

Mary Sullivan, Dawn's mentor, met with us in her office in the basement of City Hall. She has changed jobs since her days with Dawn;

she is now the city's housing director. Her office is a floating meeting with a continually changing array of participants. We had to keep moving the interview out of the way of the next meeting. The phone rang constantly. Sullivan is an earth mother in her forties who talks with everyone as if they were family members she had known forever.

When Dawn, a divorced mother of two, found herself homeless, she was given an apartment in a public housing project. Sullivan, a member of the housing staff, had encouraged Dawn to attend college. Sullivan describes herself as a "wounded healer." She is passionate about her work and wants to provide education and career opportunities to adults like Dawn in serious need of support. Sullivan's life philosophy is to help people help themselves by imparting leadership and organizational skills to her clients. However, her own road to college and career was rocky.

Sullivan's parents divorced when she was young, but her father stayed in close contact and became her hero. His beliefs were simple, derived from living through the Depression: "Pull your own weight, get a job, and pay your own way." Her parents never got any further in school than junior high school. Nonetheless, she always loved school and as a child even played games with school supplies in which she was the teacher. Sullivan was a friend to "underdogs" at school, and she always tried to bring neatness and order to the chaos she saw around her—especially at home.

With her mother, Sullivan was living in a housing project. In high school, when life got very hard, she began drinking and using drugs. She often stayed out late "to all hours" without her mother knowing or caring. Her father stepped in, put his foot down, and tried to teach her better habits. Soon after high school she eloped with a young man who tried to control her and keep her from going to college. The emerging women's movement helped her understand how tied down she would be with a child, so she avoided pregnancy and began to sneak "home courses" through correspondence over her husband's objections. The marriage ended after two years, then tragedy followed. An old boyfriend of Sullivan's committed suicide, and shortly thereafter her sister was hospitalized because of a suicide attempt.

The near-death of her sister changed Sullivan. She did not want to be a "loser"—someone who could not pull her weight—so she enrolled in a local community college. She went on to earn a bachelor's degree and then a master's degree, and she became a licensed social worker. Now Sullivan's work is aimed at helping people who are like she was. She believes that someone from a privileged background could not understand such people and could not help them as effectively. Sullivan makes sure that she lives in both worlds— the world of her past, which includes the people she works with in the housing project, and the world of educated professionals in the community. Her goal is to be a model and an advocate for the people who live in the projects.

Paul Gallo, Lela's mentor, is similar. We met in his office in the city school headquarters, where he heads the city's adult-literacy agency. His office is quiet and filled with pictures of his wife and children. However, the hallway outside his office is the human equivalent of the Indianapolis Motor Speedway, with people rushing by of every race and age.

Gallo is the local kid who made good. He is passionate about his work and feels that he understands the "reality" of adult learners—that serious disruptions often precede higher education. Gallo's parents, a factory worker and a secretary, both had high school diplomas but had not attended college. Yet they had encouraged their son's education and even managed to send him to a Catholic high school. Like most of the students at his high school, Gallo never doubted that he would go to college; his parents would have been upset if he had chosen to do otherwise. Gallo's mother drilled him on his homework, and the nuns at school helped him as well. The church had also been important to him as a child because it instilled values and ethics—something he thought was missing in the public high schools. Sometimes, Gallo had felt isolated from the kids in the neighborhood who attended the local school.

After college he was drafted, but in 1969 he chose to enlist—along with two friends—in Officer Candidate School. The three young men, destined to be officers because of their college educations, were taken to the recruiting station by their fathers, who had all been privates in World War II. The experience illustrated for Gallo how his father's dream of a better future for his son was coming true. In the army, Walter earned a master's degree in educational counseling. Gallo credits the military with teaching him how to be a leader and how to help people. It also allowed him to see a bit of the world, although he always knew he wanted to come back home.

When he had completed military service, Gallo did just that. He had studied education in college and had been an officer in the army, so he wanted a job that combined the two. In his hometown, Gallo took a new position as a counselor in the city's literacy center for adults. He left the job briefly to try a position in another community organization, but he returned to the literacy center and today is its director. Professionally, Gallo believes that he helps people by assisting them in reaching their goals. His most gratifying experiences are when students such as Lela come back to him to say hello and show him that they have made it.

The final mentor we spoke with was Anne Ryan, Billy's psychiatrist. We talked with her in her office at the city hospital. It is a small, cluttered space with paper everywhere—books lying on every surface. It looks lived in. Ryan, a single woman in her forties, is comfortably dressed and relaxed, but she behaves in a very professional manner. Of all the mentors we interviewed, she was initially the most difficult to talk with. Our questions elicited short responses from Ryan, until she became interested in the conversation itself and no longer perceived it as another academic study in which she was participating.

Anne Ryan's parents were Irish immigrants to the United States; her mother had only a second-grade education and her father had made it only through fifth grade. Ryan grew up in the Bronx and attended Catholic schools in a working-class neighborhood. Although the church is not especially important to her now, it was a central part of her life as a child. She was identified as a smart child; this pleased her parents, who in turn made Ryan feel that she was special. Her mother particularly encouraged her and took her on frequent trips to the library.

Eventually, it became "inconceivable" to Ryan that she would not attend college. Although both her parents had wanted her to go to a good Catholic college, Ryan said she always had a rebellious streak. A friend of hers had a brother at Wesleyan. They visited the campus, and she decided she would attend school there. She was a science major torn by a love of English, who decided early on to go to medical school. Her big decision was in which field she would specialize: she was divided between pathology and psychiatry. It is difficult to imagine two more different fields of study. She chose psychiatry for the human contact—Ryan likes helping people—and she joked that it would have been much more difficult to accomplish as a pathologist.

Ryan's philosophy is that people have to get on with their lives. She encourages people to go to work when they can, to be functional, to do something. She feels that additional formal education is useful only to the extent that it makes work possible.

What Makes a Mentor

Our initial observation of the nine mentors was how heterogeneous they were. We had deliberately chosen mentors who had very different types of relationships to the students—family members, teachers, and human service professionals. But the mentors were quite different from one another on other dimensions as well. They were as equally divided as to gender as nine people can be. They were a religious polyglot as well—four were Catholic, four Protestant, and one Jew. They lived all across the country—New

England, the Middle Atlantic, the Midwest, the South, and the Southwest. They had grown up in suburban, urban, and rural communities, both in and outside of the United States. They were all either white or Hispanic—notably less diverse a group than the students they mentored. Economically, they were born to both poor and privileged families, and the disparity persists today. They came from healthy as well as dysfunctional families of widely differing sizes. Their educational levels varied from no formal schooling to more than twenty years' worth. Their ages spanned from twenty-seven to sixty-six. Interestingly, the students at the selective university had the younger mentors—in large measure because family members became involved in the students' lives at much earlier ages than the service professionals met the students as adults.

We viewed this diversity as good news. It said to us that perhaps anyone can become a mentor. There do not appear to be barriers by age, gender, race, educational level, economic status, birthplace, or religion.

Yet at the same time, the mentors shared some distinctive characteristics. They had at least four attributes in common: a common worldview about the value of hard work, a belief in education as a central ingredient in success, a sense of biculturalism, and a belief that they could make a difference. First, they all spoke the same language and shared a common worldview. The mentors were latter-day Horatio Algers. Every one of them espoused the same values that Alger had: not so much luck as pluck and hard work. They put it this way:

> "I think I am all the time happy . . . working hard makes me happy."   (Helen Barrientos)

> "I never think I'm going to have two cars. I never think I'm going to have a house. I never think I'm going to have money. I have [these things now]. I never think I'm going to be that much in my life. I just keep working every day, and every morning I say thank you God for giving me another day and for giving me a chance."   (Carlos Gomez)

"You have a certain survival mechanism when you grow up in rural areas. You have a certain independence. . . . You learn to survive. . . . You find a way to entertain yourself. You find a way to pay for college. You find a way to pay for going to the prom. . . . You didn't have an environment that was conducive to giving you things. . . . You had to provide it for yourself . . . get in the self-sufficiency mode."   (Karen Gilman)

"That was the culture of the area. . . . You worked."
(Karen Gilman)

"You need to work for what you get. There is opportunity out there. . . . Well, here's the way you do it: go through high school, do well, get into college, and get a job."
(Margaret Wilson)

"I'm a product of the Depression era. . . . It instilled in me that you'd better get a job and it better be secure because there is nothing worse than being unemployed."
(David Goodman)

"I like to work hard."   (Bob Anderson)

"I didn't want to be a loser. To me, a loser was like if you didn't pull your own weight and have your own good job."
(Mary Sullivan)

"Grow up and get a real job and be an adult."
(Mary Sullivan)

"Just pave my own way in life and don't be dependent on other people."   (Mary Sullivan)

"I always worked."   (Paul Gallo)

"People have to work. My job is to get them to work."
(Anne Ryan)

Each of the nine mentors believed that hard work was the cornerstone of success. Without exception, they thought that if you worked hard you would thrive. Even Helen Barrientos, who had so very little, attributed what she did have in life and how far she had come, to her long hours and diligence as a hospital technician and a mother.

Underlying this common belief was an idealism about the future. All nine mentors believed that tomorrow could be better than today, that the system works, that the American Dream lives, and that any person who wants to can succeed in the United States. All that it takes is hard work.

A second characteristic the mentors shared was a belief that the level of an individual's success in life is tied to his or her education. For the mentors, education was the social equivalent of religion. Despite the many ways that one could be a "success" in American society—a wealthy business entrepreneur, a professional athlete, a film star—the mentors put their faith in education instead. And they conveyed that faith to the students whose lives they touched. They did not encourage the students to get jobs, for example, so that they might save money to become venture capitalists. Neither the students nor mentors we interviewed told the kinds of success stories that had been so popular at the turn of the century—stories of men such as Andrew Carnegie, who had boasted about his penchant for making millions despite his complete *lack* of formal education.

> "When I asked for a raise . . . I didn't get [it] . . . because I wasn't certified. . . . They always said, 'Oh well, we can't give you as high a position' or whatever, because I didn't have the piece of paper . . . I think to make a better life you have to be educated. You have to go to college . . . to live a better life than me."   (Helen Barrientos, as translated by her daughter Maria)

> "I didn't want [Maria] to suffer as much as I had to suffer or go through similar hardship. So when I saw that she had the

opportunity or the desire to study at a university, I encouraged her."   (Helen Barrientos, as translated by her daughter Maria)

"I am never interested in money. I am more interested in learning."   (Helen Barrientos, as translated by her daughter Maria)

"I believe in education. I believe in the people. I believe in . . . to teach the people."   (Carlos Gomez)

"The people need to be prepared for everything. . . . I believe in the preparation of the people, girls or men or whatever; you need preparation for everything."   (Carlos Gomez)

"So, you have a lot of chances to win and be prepared."
(Carlos Gomez)

"I guess [going to school] was the only time I felt stable and secure and normal.   (Karen Gilman)

"[E]ducation is the way out."   (Karen Gilman)

"I think I believed education was important. And maybe that was ground into me. But it really was."   (Margaret Wilson)

"Education is the key for my kids."   (David Goodman)

"[E]ducation is the answer."   (Bob Anderson)

"Every time I learned something, I would get excited about learning something new. . . . And there was something about that that gave me hope for the future. I don't exactly understand the mechanism, but I guess I knew that this was narrow, and that there was more out there and I was gonna get there eventually."   (Mary Sullivan)

"I just knew that college was out there and I was limited where I was. . . . I was frustrated. So did I know anybody who [went] to college? Probably on TV."   (Mary Sullivan)

"And we all know, I know, you know . . . that you keep getting your education taken care of . . . and opportunity becomes almost—not boundless and limitless, but you can do a lot [more] difficult things than you think would be possible."
(Paul Gallo)

Anne Ryan differed somewhat from the others in that she did not see education as a panacea. Her preference was for work over education. She recommended that her patients get jobs. Ryan's highest priority was that her patients become functional. Only when they were incapable of working did Ryan suggest education. Nonetheless, in talking about her own life, Ryan said that education was what had made her life better than her parents'. It gave her two generations of social mobility—taking her from a working-class life to a career in psychiatry, bypassing a typical intermediate step of an entry-level professional job.

For all the mentors, if education was not synonymous with social mobility, it was at least the trigger. Every one of them accepted the old maxim that the more you learn, the more you earn; several probably would add an asterisk indicating that the learning had to be certified or marked by degrees. The two mentors with the least amount of formal education—Helen Barrientos and Carlos Gomez—drove home the value of education repeatedly. They were at once didactic and proselytizing. Carlos Gomez in particular had developed his own education sermon, which he gave again and again in the course of our interview. He was a true believer, but so were all the rest. He was simply more explicit and less subtle.

The mentors saw education as giving people far more than economic power. They talked about personal growth and development, although they rarely used such jargon. They spoke of the role of education in preparing people for a better life in the broadest sense of the term. Gomez explained his realizations in a very touching way. He said that although he now had money, whenever he went downtown to talk to doctors or lawyers they still saw him as a nobody. He didn't talk right. He didn't act right. He didn't dress right. What he lacked was education. The other mentors and Gomez himself would have argued that education was the remedy. The road to social, economic, and personal success for them was paved with education.

The third attribute the mentors shared was biculturalism. At some level, every one of them knew about the life of poor and disadvantaged people, as well as the world of the advantaged and educated. Not only were the mentors conversant in other cultures, they seemed to straddle the two worlds. Mary Sullivan described herself this way:

> "I think in the general sense of the word I fit in almost anywhere I go. I think I've learned a lot how to play out different hands—when to walk and when to fold. In general, I don't look up or down, so I can fit in with people who make the rules, as well as [with] people who break them."

Each of the mentors had come to comprehend a world in which he or she did not live. Along with that comprehension came an understanding of what it took to traverse the two worlds. However, the mentors were not necessarily comfortable in both worlds. Carlos Gomez made it clear that he did not fit in with professionals. Anne Ryan was, in some respects, the most distant from the poor people she served. And Mary Sullivan sometimes felt uncomfortable in both worlds.

> "When sometimes . . . I'm working with people who are struggling in their journey and I'm ahead of them, so to speak, I feel a little funny about that. I don't want to stand out. I'll help them but I don't want the fanfare kind of thing. I wouldn't want them to call me like Ma'am or Miss and all this stuff. And by the same token—I don't quite know why sometimes . . . I am [un]comfortable with other professionals. . . . I had a

school committee meeting with some people and I was a little intimidated. At first, I thought it was maybe 'cause they
were higher up the ladder than me, and then I thought, it was
maybe 'cause I didn't trust them."

The mentors had acquired their biculturalism in different ways.
Karen Gilman, David Goodman, Bob Anderson, Mary Sullivan,
Paul Gallo, and Anne Ryan had made the journey themselves from
one culture to the other. Other mentors—Helen Barrientos, Carlos
Gomez, and Margaret Wilson—had not.

Barrientos and Gomez learned about the life of educated and
affluent people by meeting them. Barrientos worked among the doctors in a hospital. She talked to them and observed the differences
between their lives and hers. She learned what they had and how
they got it.

Gomez, too, had encountered educated people on the job: his
employers at the Mexican bullring were college-educated. Also, he
had a friend from the community where he had grown up who
became an engineer. Gomez said, "I peeked into the minds of educated people."

"They went to college and they were better off.

"And I saw the difference. I saw the difference because they had
a lot of chance to do what they want to do and we don't. . . .
We don't have a title and then nobody recognizes us.

"And nobody, no matter how much I know, I'm going to be the
same thing."

Like Helen Barrientos and Carlos Gomez, most of the mentors
had learned about the "other culture" by propinquity or contact. For
Karen Gilman and Margaret Wilson, this exposure came through
travel. Gilman had traveled throughout the United States as a
baton twirler. It was an eye-opening experience for her.

"I knew that there was a climate and an environment and a city or a town that was more fun, where I had more opportunities, more people to meet, where [I] didn't have to know everybody and their grandmother. It . . . was just a chance to . . . start over."

Wilson, who came from a missionary family and had married into one, said she loved to travel. She was "fascinated by other cultures and getting to know people from other cultures." Wilson felt that this was probably why she was "attracted to people of other ethnic backgrounds"—such as the youngsters who had lived in her home as foster children.

Two of the men attributed their glimpse at "others" to their stints in the military. For David Goodman and Paul Gallo, the army had shown them a very different side of life.

School was another venue for meeting people from other cultures. When Anne Ryan attended college at Wesleyan, she met a group of students unlike any she had ever known. They were far more affluent and lived very different lives from hers. She "found a whole other world." Mary Sullivan had the same experience in high school. Going from her neighborhood junior high school to the citywide high school, she encountered extremes in students' backgrounds that she had never before imagined.

There was another, less direct, way that the mentors learned about other cultures: they heard and read about them. Books had been an important part of growing up for several of the mentors—Helen Barrientos, Carlos Gomez, Bill Anderson, David Goodman, Mary Sullivan, and Anne Ryan. It was Barrientos who described most vividly what she had learned not only from reading books but also from watching television. She had lived near the home of a distant relative's family in Colombia and would baby-sit for their child. They had a television, and Barrientos would watch it all the time. They also had books, and she would read them—especially the biology books. These experiences taught her "that people who are educated have a wider vocabulary . . . their manners are more refined, [they have] broader visions, and they're more open-minded." Books and television introduced her to a world she didn't know existed.

The mentors also mentioned church as a place where they learned about the needs of other people. The church played an integral part in the lives of six of the mentors, and it had the most direct influence on Margaret Wilson:

> [My husband and I] went to a church program where someone from . . . child welfare, I guess it was, came and talked about the need for foster parents. And we said, well, you know we'll sign up. And lo and behold, the first foster [child] we got was a sixteen-year-old [girl] and she lived with us for six months.

What really stood out about the biculturalism of all the mentors is that they had all arrived at the same place but had taken very different routes to get there.

The fourth attribute the mentors shared was a belief that they could make a difference—and a commitment to doing so.

> "She always wanted me to work and become educated, not so that I would . . . become rich or famous or whatever, but she wanted me to become useful to my society, and that's the most important thing: to do something that helps somebody. (Maria, talking about her mother, Helen Barrientos)

> "My mother's attitude toward children is to teach: 'They're little plants; they grow and grow, you water them, and you add lots of fertilizer.'"   (Maria, talking about her mother, Helen Barrientos)

> "One thing in my life is to help the people." (Carlos Gomez)

"I mean my whole goal is to not only make a difference for people right now, but to teach them things that are going to affect them for eternity, and to really let my life reflect Christ and his work through me. I don't believe it is just a matter of 'Get all the toys you can and then you die and the one with the most toys wins.' That is not what it's all about at all. It's about affecting not only now, but long-term, after you die, where you go. So I guess [that] really what I'm all about is making a difference."   (Karen Gilman)

[Wilson and her husband] "enjoy maybe helping people. . . . When you're a missionary's kid . . . you're kind of taught to deny yourself. Maybe I don't deserve what I have. I mean, neither one of us thought we would have as much as we have. And so the family was kind of given to service . . . and what we can do to make the world a better place."   (Margaret Wilson)

"I help kids. I give them a second chance."
(Bob Anderson)

"I'm a saver."   (Mary Sullivan)

"I'm a wounded healer . . . something happened to you along the way and maybe someone helped you out, and with me it stuck."   (Mary Sullivan)

"[My goal is to] help others help themselves so they can be experienced, [be] happier, [and] lead fuller, productive lives . . . and 'productive' can be what they want it to be. Productive could mean a smile, could mean money, could mean food on the table. Whatever productive means to them."
(Mary Sullivan)

"I love what I'm doing . . . I really feel like what I do makes a difference. I feel like I've been able to help create something

that's respected and that's honored now that wasn't before—
the work of educators—and that [gives me] immediate grati-
fication. I see people who are successful who graduate, change
their lives."   (Paul Gallo)

"I change people."   (Anne Ryan)

It would be a mistake to conclude that these mentors are a
bunch of wild-eyed social activists. Rather, what came through
clearly in the interviews was a quieter sense of confidence and commitment. The mentors knew the problems their students faced; they
understood how to help the students overcome them; they believed
they had the skills to assist the students; and they were committed
to doing so.

And this brings us to the most unexpected finding of our interviews with the mentors. They each assisted their "mentees" in different ways. There was no one approach to their work and no
general formula about the sequence of actions they took. The mentors' approaches could be classified as autobiographical—that is, the
mentors sought to copy what had worked in their own lives and to
avoid passing on what had not. The professionals added to this
approach a body of theory and practice in their fields of expertise.

In this sense, the mentors were not interchangeable: Billy's therapist, for example, could not substitute for Maria's mother. Each
mentor had crafted an individualized escape route based on his or
her own strengths and weaknesses and the perceived needs of the
student.

On the other hand, the mentors were exactly alike in another
respect: although they took different approaches and engaged in
varied activities, they had similar ideas and shared common perspectives. For example, they thought biculturally. They felt that
they could make a difference in the lives of disadvantaged people,
and they were committed to doing so. They believed that education

was the key to social mobility and that the American Dream was alive and well.

The job of the mentors was to apply this perspective to the lives of the individuals they served. In this sense, the perspectives of Maria's mother and Billy's therapist were the same. Their "philosophies" were interchangeable, even while their personas were not.

In the final analysis, the mentor interviews didn't show us the road map of actions that are necessary to fashion an escape route— we really learned that from the students they assisted. Instead, the mentors showed us what it took to become a mentor. Their stories leave us with a design for creating new mentors. It tells us that the characteristics that mentors share are learned rather than innate. And it shows us that perhaps anyone can have the capacity to become a mentor.

7

The Lesson

One Arm Around One Child

The most important lesson of this book is that many, many more poor people can go to college than are currently attending. Race, gender, religion, and birthplace need not be barriers.

In the simplest terms, the recipe for getting to college is mentorship—one arm around one child; one mentor with one poor person. This chapter gives us some useful insight into the most advantageous placement of the arm.

Focus on Young People

In this book, the key difference in how students arrived at college was the difference in their ages. Older adults had a much more difficult time getting to college than did students of traditional college age, eighteen to twenty-two. In general, the older students brought more troubled pasts and less supportive relationships to their college experiences. They came with lower levels of confidence and greater doubts about their intellectual abilities. They possessed little knowledge—but a great deal of misinformation—about higher education. They had made lives for themselves that did not require a college education. Their friends, relatives, and co-workers had generally not attended college. It took major disruptions in their lives—divorces, illnesses, or immigration—to get them to apply to college. Once they were enrolled, higher education created further disjunctions in their existing relationships.

For younger students, the path to college was much smoother and the transition more natural—particularly if there was no interruption in their schooling. The younger students came with less historical and emotional baggage. Although college also disrupted their relationships, it did not do so to the degree experienced by the older students.

In addition, the mechanisms for directing poor people to college were more readily identifiable and potent to young people than to the older adults. This book has shown that families and schools have had the largest impact on getting young people to college. Most youngsters are intimately connected with these institutions prior to higher education and are therefore receptive to their influences. For older adults, there is no analog; for the most part, they get to college through the much more diffuse web of human-services or other helping agencies. In this sense, the adults are much more widely dispersed, with few common entry points or anchors prior to their transition to college.

In the course of writing this book, we asked adult education experts around the country about the existence of programs to promote college access for poor adults. Almost invariably, the educators failed to understand the question. They cited programs that primarily emphasized literacy, vocational training, continuing education, or professional development—but not college. They often named the armed forces and the prisons as the principal providers of education for low-income adults.

In offering this analysis and stressing that intervention efforts should be targeted at young kids, we are not saying that adults should be ignored or overlooked. However, we are convinced that current programs are not working for them. We are simply saying that adults are much more difficult to recruit to college, that the price they pay for recruitment is much higher, and that the first chances at college are easier and more effective than the second chances and that the transition to college is easier and more successful if the student is of traditional college age. As a nation, we need to do better in making college available for poor adults. Our hope is that by targeting young people, the number of poor adults who make up this much more diffuse recruitment population would be reduced.

Start Early

This book shows that the earlier in school we begin preparing young people for college, the easier their transition to college—and the greater the opportunities available to them. Admission to a selective university requires early preparation. In fact, the selective university we studied was even less open to the poor than we had imagined. Earlier, we stressed that being admitted to a selective school was not at all like being discovered sitting on a stool in a Hollywood drugstore and then going on to stardom. In reality, almost all of the poor students we interviewed at the selective university had been involved since childhood in the academic equivalent of acting classes, summer stock, road companies, and regional theater prior to being "discovered" by the selective university. To drop the metaphor, the poor students had been tested for years and years before applying to the selective university. Their childhoods had been filled with enrichment activities, and they had already been proven performers prior to admission. They had followed a rigorous common regimen to prepare for the university.

In this sense, the selective university was not a risk taker. It did not often take a chance on the unknown valedictorian at an inner-city ghetto high school or on the salutatorian at a rural secondary school. Only two of the students we interviewed fit into this category: Jenny and Lester. For most poor people, being admitted to the selective university required action in elementary or middle school. It is highly unlikely that a poor person could, in the last year of high school, decide and prepare to attend the selective university; by that time, it is too late. The student would not have undertaken the requisite enrichment activities or testing required for admission.

In contrast, it is difficult to imagine an institution more open to the poor than the community college. Many of the students we interviewed had come to the two-year college with horrendous academic records, and many had dropped out of high school. For many, the years following school had brought few successes and much pain. The two-year college was open to all of these students. Beyond finances, the biggest barrier they faced in attending the community college was personal fear. Whereas the biggest barriers for the poor at the selective university were imposed by the institution itself—interviews and admissions criteria—the greatest barriers at the community college were often created by the students. They were simply afraid to apply or attend. Their lack of early preparation was a liability for both the students and their colleges.

Early identification as a child with potential made the path to college far easier for students. The transition for young people was gradual and continuous—filled with enrichment activities along the way—while for older adults it could be disruptive and sudden. In fact, it was so natural for the youngsters that few of them at the selective college realized that their life trajectory had changed. This is why so many of them honestly thought they had decided on attending a selective college in their senior year of high school; they forgot that they had been groomed for the choice since childhood. When preparation for college for poor youngsters begins early, the students have the capacity to go further with greater ease.

Think Locally

The path from poverty to higher education is constructed in the poor student's community or neighborhood. All the mentors we interviewed lived or worked near the students they assisted.

Although many of the students had taken advantage of government programs to attend college or had experienced enrichment events outside their communities, these actions were supplementary—their path to college began locally. It was rooted in the neighborhood and in the local institutions.

Plan Individually

The process by which poor people come to attend college is an individual rather than mass phenomenon. In the language of the marketplace, it is retail, not wholesale, work in the sense that it requires intensive involvement with individuals rather than passing contact with larger numbers.

The actors in the process have been remarkably constant for all the students—a poor person and one or more mentors. For more than a century—from the work of Jacob Riis to that of William J. Wilson—scores of influential books and reports have been published on the complex pathology of poverty. In light of this body of work, which depicts poverty as virtually intractable, it is startling to realize that one individual can make the difference in whether or not a poor person goes to college. All but two of the students we interviewed attributed their decision to attend college to a special person or mentor. Younger students at the selective university cited mentors who came principally from the primary social institutions in the lives of children—families and schools. The older students at the community college were more likely to find mentors in secondary or safety-net institutions, including therapists and human-services providers. As a result, mentors differed dramatically both in what they knew about higher education and in the time they spent with the students. While, ironically, the mentors of the two-year college students tended to know more about higher education than did the mentors of the university students, the university mentors spent more time with the students than did the community college mentors. Also, the mentors of the selective university students began working with them at younger ages.

In the end, each of the mentors had accomplished the same four things—imparting hope, building confidence, communicating the importance of education, and bringing potential students and colleges together. However, every one of the mentors did this in a different way. Each created a path to college based upon the needs of the person needing assistance and the strengths and weaknesses the mentor brought to the relationship. What could be more different than the approaches used by Billy's therapist and Maria's mother?

At the same time, it is important to note that both the approach the mentor used and the role he or she held (parent, teacher, therapist, and so on) might work at a particular point in a person's life but not at other times. Indeed, college had been suggested to several of the community college students in their youth, but they had rejected the suggestion. Barry was a perfect example: he had considered higher education only when both his mentor and his life circumstances changed.

Create Enrichment Experiences, Minimize Risks

Regardless of which approach each of the mentors took, they tried to steer students away from the lures of the war zone. Maria's mother had done this in the most pointed fashion. She would drop Maria off at school moments before the bell rang, and she would pick her up at school right after classes let out; she even brought her along to work. Maria would do her homework sitting beside her mother. Weekends would be filled with activities designed to keep Maria off the streets.

At the same time, the mentors sought to improve the students' positions through enrichment activities. Brenda, for example, had attended a private school, spent her summer at an elite academy, traveled widely, and engaged in a panoply of extracurricular activities.

Make Use of Accelerating Institutions

Two very different kinds of institutions had the effect of substantially improving the students' chances of attending college. For the younger students, the institution was the selective preparatory school. For the older adults, it was the military.

Build the Mentor Team

Many of the people interviewed for this book had a single mentor, but others were served by a number of them, even though one mentor would be dominant in their lives. Expanding the mentor group gave the students a wider range of expertise from which to draw support and knowledge. For example, Anita's teachers had passed her along one to another and from grade to grade. Each year the group of supportive teachers had been enlarged, and all of them had remained available and helpful to Anita. Brenda added different types of people to her group of mentors—a teacher, a debate coach, a guidance counselor, and others. Each brought additional knowledge and skills to building Brenda's path to college.

Encourage Everyone to Become a Mentor

The mentors were a diverse group in terms of race, religion, socioeconomic status, education, age, geography, background, and just about any other criteria one can imagine. The implication is that a broad range of individuals have the capacity to serve as mentors to poor people. For youngsters, the most effective mentors were people who had been poor themselves. The only prerequisites we identified were optimism about the future, a belief in education, biculturalism, and a desire to make a difference.

These findings raise the question of how mentorship can be effectively spread. Given the power and simplicity of the tool, how can more poor people be exposed to it? How can individuals who may not recognize their mentoring skills be alerted to the possibility? How can people in the most likely positions to serve as mentors become willing and prepared to accept that role?

If our focus is indeed on young people as the group most available for mobility between poverty and college, this requires targeting the relatives—particularly parents—and teachers of disadvantaged children to serve as mentors. Creating formal mentor-development programs, which would teach potential mentors about the power of education, would be a worthwhile goal. Through guest speakers and field visits, such programs could give participants the bicultural experiences they need, as well as encourage potential mentors to gain a sense of efficacy by apprenticing in existing mentorships and by meeting others like themselves. Such programs could be developed in any school or neighborhood institution; all they would require is a little money, some time, and interest.

Evening the Odds

Making College Possible for the Poor

Today, individual institutions, the federal government, private philanthropy, state and local governments, and community groups all play some role in keeping college accessible to the poor. Yet as a nation, we have no clear or unified policy toward higher education for the poor and no commonly agreed upon conception of what works best. What we do have is several decades' worth of experiments, initiatives, programs, and laws, each of which has taught us something new. Learning from the strengths and weaknesses of the past and building upon them, we are evolving toward programs that may work for large numbers of poor people using the best of what we learned in the course of writing this book.

Several mechanisms have been employed in the past to increase college access for the poor—special institutions, government initiatives, intervention programs, and financial aid, to name but a few. This chapter looks at three major initiatives designed to help poor people attend college: special colleges for the poor, federal financial aid programs, and various intervention programs aimed at poor youngsters. We then take a close look at what we consider the most exciting program. Interestingly, it is a program that already follows many of the lessons gleaned from our twenty-four–student study and that utilizes what appears to be the most potent way of reaching the very poor: early intervention by a mentor.

Colleges for the Poor

Efforts by colleges and universities to make higher education accessible to the poor are not new. As illustrated in Chapter Two, it started with the founding of Harvard University in the seventeenth century. Yet in the past, most institutions were passive: they did not seek out the poor, but did accept the few who found their way to the college's doorstep. Most institutions that had started with such a commitment gave it up as they became more prosperous and mainstream. The number of institutions that maintained their commitment to the poor is relatively small.

One of the more distinctive features of the American system of higher education is the establishment of colleges dedicated to serving specific student populations. For the most part, these institutions can be viewed as remedial initiatives—responses to the absence of collegiate access for particular groups of people. The founding of women's colleges, for example, was a reaction to a largely or exclusively male system of higher education. Catholic and Jewish colleges were established in response to discrimination by a system of higher education created by Protestant sects. And historically black and tribal colleges were created to counteract barriers imposed by a system run by white people.

Institutions for the poor came into being in the same fashion. Their establishment was initially a reaction to the lack of higher education for poor people in the decades before the Civil War. The result was as assortment of different types of schools. There were colleges for laborers in the fields and factories, such as the Peoples College, the Farmers College, and later, Brookwood Labor College. Institutions such as the Free Academy in New York City sprang up for the urban poor, and schools such as Highlander Folk College and Berea College were established for the rural poor, with a shared focus on Appalachia.

This genre of colleges might be described as shadow institutions:

they not only existed in the shadows of the established colleges, but they also were less substantial reflections of those institutions at the time they were created. Because they enrolled poor people, these colleges were often poor themselves. Because their students had little previous education, these schools seldom offered instruction at the collegiate level. Because they sought out excluded groups who did not require a college education for their work or their lives, these schools had small student bodies. And because they appeared to be so radical in politics, philosophy, and student body and represented such a broad departure from traditional practice, they were often short-lived, failing to attract adequate enrollments or sufficient philanthropic support.

These institutions sprang up like weeds and were often unconnected with one another; they were products of an idea or a conviction. Most of them failed. Frequently, they were established before there was a real demand for what they offered. As soon as one institution failed, another was created to carry out the same task. But this was not the fate of all such colleges. Some survived and even thrived, transforming themselves into traditional institutions and bringing groups of poor students into the mainstream of higher education. This is what happened to the historically black colleges, for example.

Today, a number of these institutions designed for the poor survive around the country. We have chosen to look at two of them that represent opposite extremes in the educational spectrum. Hostos Community College is an open-admission two-year school that opened its doors in the South Bronx in New York City in 1970; its students are principally older adults. Berea College is a selective four-year liberal arts school in Kentucky that was founded in 1859; it focuses largely on students of traditional college age.

Hostos Community College is set in the poorest congressional district in the United States. It enrolls a student body that does not typically attend college—the hard-core poor. In fact, of the 5,400 students attending Hostos, 80 percent are Hispanic. Nearly all of them (92 percent) live below the poverty line, and 82 percent have family incomes of less than $8,000 per year.

A majority of the students at Hostos (63 percent) are single heads of households with dependent children; 75 percent are women. The average age of the students is thirty. Less than 20 percent come directly from high school, and 33 percent have GEDs.

Hostos sets three goals for itself: to use bilingual education as a means of removing linguistic barriers to higher education; to offer career and technical programs that lead to employment and socio-economic mobility; and to provide knowledge and critical-thinking skills through the study of liberal arts for transfer to a senior college, for professional advancement, and for life.

These goals translate into a unique program. Hostos offers degrees in the traditional community-college fields—liberal arts, allied health, and business. It also has certificate programs in areas such as word processing. Both the professional and vocational offerings are tied to the labor market of the local community.

However, Hostos offers more than academic programs. It also provides services geared to the needs of a poor Hispanic community. Counseling and support services are essential: since most of the students have never before attended college (and never expected to), special efforts through orientation programs are critical to helping students feel good about themselves and understand what college is all about. The Hostos library, for example, has been turned into a study center of sorts. It contains only a small collection of books—52,000 volumes—but it has become a refuge for students.

Hostos has extended its services directly into the local neighborhood. There are advisory committees of residents and employers. The college has built ties with young people by creating activity programs for children from the primary grades through high school. It has extended its involvement down through the school system, having opened its facilities to house a middle school.

In contrast to Hostos, Berea College has the look of the quintes-
sential New England college campus—brick as far as the eye can see,
quadrangles, tree-lined paths, and the obligatory assortment of dogs.

Berea's endowment of more than $350 million makes it the fifty-
first wealthiest college in the country. It has a traditional liberal arts
curriculum and strongly encourages residential life; over 90 percent
of the students live on campus. It receives top rankings in national
college surveys such as *The Selective Guide to Colleges* and the *U.S.
News and World Report* list of best colleges. And most important,
Berea offers the kind of college experience that has historically been
out of the reach of poor people.

At Berea, all of this is *only* for the poor—"for students whose
families would have a difficult time financing a college education
without assistance." The students are financially disadvantaged but
academically able. Of Berea's almost 1,500 students, half come from
families making less than $16,000 per year, and 81 percent were in
the top two-fifths of their high school graduating class. College pub-
lications are filled with accounts of dirt-poor students who brought
potatoes, butter and eggs, chickens and pigs, green beans and
molasses to barter for an education; of two brothers who walked "a
hundred miles" to Berea leading a cow, hoping to put themselves
through college by selling its milk, and of a twenty-year-old boy who
arrived with little more than 60 cents in his pocket.

Berea charges no tuition. All fees—except for room, board, and
expenses—were eliminated in 1892. To assist students in meeting
the additional costs, the college has offered a labor program since
its founding. All students are required to work at least ten hours a
week; this pays for between 20 and 60 percent of a term bill. The
notion of service is also key to the Berea philosophy. The college is
committed to the advancement of the people of southern
Appalachia (defined as all of Kentucky and 228 counties in eight
other states).

This combination of philosophy, program, and people committed to the mission of Berea produces unusually positive results.

Slightly more than half of the students who enter Berea complete a degree and more than half of the graduates go on to professional or graduate schools. Most students return to live and work in Appalachia. This is a very high baccalaureate completion and graduate school attendance rate for disadvantaged youngsters.

Part of the reason for Berea's successful graduation rates is that Berea minimizes the cultural clash experienced by the poor at other selective colleges. Berea students come from families that in the main do not understand college, how it works, and the role it plays in social mobility. The families frequently do not encourage their children's aspirations. Berea provides motivation and support to these students. Beyond this, Berea's environment cushions the students against the alienness typically found in the selective college. The homogeneity in backgrounds of the student body eliminates the economic and cultural disparity that poor students typically find at selective schools.

But the importance of Berea goes far beyond the fact that its students earn degrees. Young people experience dramatic growth during the college years. Study after study of Berea students shows that they have greater flexibility, increased self-esteem and confidence, a more liberal intellectual orientation, increased cognitive and affective complexity, high moral development, and more. The effect is evident in the students' postcollege plans, too: Berea students take two jumps in social and economic mobility. This is in stark contrast to most poor students who attend nonresidential two-year colleges and receive vocational training rather than a liberal arts education. This is a distinct liability for both educational achievement and life attainment (Astin, 1985; Brint and Karabel, 1989; Chickering, 1974).

In summary, the success of Berea reaffirms the lessons of Hostos, and the same conditions that increased access at Hostos apply to Berea as well. The qualities that matter in these colleges are commitment, leadership, appropriate programs, a supportive environment, community outreach, a staff to match the needs of the students, and effective recruitment. But currently Berea goes a step further: it shows that for poor but able students, attending a traditionally selective college—and reaping the rewards of such an education—are possible.

Berea and Hostos are extraordinary institutions. They can certainly teach the higher-education establishment a great deal about effectively educating the poor. These two colleges, and institutions like them, are undeniably successful in helping poor students beat the odds. Structurally, however, they are unable to materially change the odds against poor students as a class.

Colleges for the poor are most effective in assisting the economically disadvantaged in overcoming the second of the two barriers they face—getting into college—rather than the first, which is getting out of a poor neighborhood. The colleges provide warm, inviting, and educationally well-planned environments for their poor students. As examples of colleges for the poor in general, Hostos and Berea were supportive of their students. Yet, neither college was able to overcome the opposition to, or lack of understanding of, college that students frequently faced at home, nor was either able to address all the financial needs of its students. Most important, the number of students served by Berea and Hostos and all other colleges for the poor is very small. Such institutions do not have the capacity to reach more than a sprinkling of the entire population of disadvantaged students.

The real weakness of utilizing colleges for the poor as a means of opening higher education to the disadvantaged, however, is that they are unable to respond meaningfully to the first barrier that poor people face. Almost by definition, colleges for the poor cannot apply all the lessons gleaned from our study. For example, they do not focus on children. Despite community-outreach efforts, Berea's target audience is older teenagers, while Hostos reaches mostly adults. For the same reasons, the colleges cannot reach the kids early or build a mentor team for kids. Neither college regularly touches the lives of elementary school students, nor does it touch the lives of the men and women likely to be the children's mentors—their parents and teachers. Both institutions do emphasize locality, however. Hostos, which makes use of innovative recruitment and admission procedures, even offers enrichment programs to precollege-age students through a middle school on its campus.

Yet the efforts of these schools cannot be termed systematic. They touch too few people. The inescapable conclusions are that colleges for the poor make a very large difference in the lives of the students they serve, and that such schools have a lot to teach other institutions about how to better educate the poor. However, they are not the solution for substantially increasing the odds of college access for poor people.

Financial Aid

If creating special colleges for the poor, where tuition and fees are low or nonexistent, cannot systematically address the needs of poor people, another strategy that the country has been engaged in in varying degrees since the 1960s—providing poor students money to attend college where they choose—may provide a further solution. Interestingly, much of current financial aid policy is based on lessons learned from a program that was not explicitly designed as such—the Servicemen's Readjustment Act of 1944, more commonly known as the G.I. Bill.

The G.I. Bill produced some startling revelations about higher education in America. The first was that there was a huge and untapped demand for college—much larger than ever imagined. On the eve of World War II, 1.5 million students were attending college. The G.I. Bill was anticipated to bring perhaps another few hundred thousand students to the nation's campuses. The fact that 2.2 million veterans actually took advantage of the opportunity was a shock to both higher education and the government.

The second revelation was that financial aid was the key to unlocking the demand for college education—40 percent of returning World War II veterans took advantage of the G.I. Bill. The enormous drawing power of scholarship money was unanticipated.

A third revelation was that nontraditional students could be successful in college. The higher-education community was convinced that the worldly former G.I.'s would not only corrupt traditional undergraduates but would be unable to compete with them academically. Just the opposite occurred, however. In general, married G.I.'s with children achieved the highest grades. Next came married G.I.'s without children, followed by unmarried G.I.'s. Traditional students brought up the rear (Levine, A., 1989a).

These revelations laid the foundations for financial aid programs, which were established beginning in the 1960s. They were premised on the belief that large numbers of able students both wanted to attend and could succeed in college but lacked the resources to do so. Financial aid was seen as the engine necessary for opening higher education to them. As Chapter Two showed, these assumptions were only partially correct. Their limits have been tested through four decades of national financial aid policy, and a raft of studies have been carried out on the effectiveness of that policy.

One of the more comprehensive studies was undertaken in 1988 by Larry Leslie and Paul Brinkman. They asked whether need-based financial aid removed economic barriers to college and gave students of equal ability an equal opportunity to participate in higher education. Recognizing that no comprehensive national database on financial aid exists, the authors took three different analytic approaches to their question. They examined econometric analyses of financial aid, student perceptions of aid, and participation-rate studies of college attendance.

In summary, Leslie and Brinkman were unable to discern the true effect of financial aid on access to higher education by low-income students. In the studies they examined, they encountered differing methodologies and samples and a lack of control over intervening variables. Despite these methodological weaknesses, however, they were able to conclude more grossly that while financial aid has encouraged an increase in the enrollment rates of low-income students, particularly in community colleges, larger disparities remain in the college participation rates of low- and high-income families today than when the federal financial aid programs began.

Most other studies of financial aid have produced similar results. The bottom line is that financial aid is a necessary but insufficient condition for college attendance by the poor.

The weaknesses of the current federal financial aid program in its ability to systematically help the poor include the complexity of the process, the lack of information by students, and the fluctuation in funds available. Critics argue that flaws in the program's design— particularly the difficulty of the application process—make it far less effective than it could be in helping the poor attend college. The forms are complex and technically demanding, require educational sophistication, and ask students to report financial information that can be either embarrassing or impossible to provide. Poor Hispanic males, in particular, have been ashamed to report wages (Boston Higher Education Center; conversation with Ann Coles, 1992). Illegal immigrants and those without green cards are often afraid to answer financial questions as well.

Poor students frequently lack sufficient financial aid information, and this is an enormous problem. Many high school seniors are ignorant of the various types of financial aid available; for poor students, this is a major barrier. For example, a 1989 study of Indiana high school seniors found that only half could identify four of the six federal financial aid programs (National Commission on Responsibilities for Financing Postsecondary Education, 1993, pp. 15, 16). Yet, this was a study of the general student population. Poor students and their families often know even less about financial aid and college costs than does the general public (Dixon, 1988, pp. 29–36).

In our study, the poor students of traditional college age who were attending a selective university had managed to gain a sophisticated understanding of financial aid. In contrast, the students attending two-year schools often did so with very limited knowledge of financial aid. Indeed, we encountered students in our study who dropped out of the community colleges for lack of very small amounts of money—car fare to and from school. If these students had to leave school for such small sums, it is likely that significant numbers have failed to enroll for similar amounts.

For older students, federal financial aid poses the largest obstacles. Current programs are designed for financially dependent young people, without spouses and children, who attend college full-time. However, nontraditional students already constitute a majority of the college population, and they represent the fastest-growing group in higher education (Levine, A., 1989b). Current financial aid programs do not pay adequate attention to differences in the financial resources of poor independent students; the academic progress rates of older students requiring remediation; and the additional expenses associated with having a family (such as day care). Increased information on financial aid is a necessity for older as well as younger students heading for both expensive and low-cost colleges.

Another common criticism concerns the amount of financial aid available. Government funding levels have been erratic, yo-yoing up and down and making financial aid an undependable resource for college support for the poor (Hauptman, 1991). The nature of financial aid has also shifted dramatically in the past fifteen years from grants to loans. In 1971, grants made up 66 percent of all federal aid, and loans made up 29 percent. By 1991, loans had increased to over 60 percent of aid, while grants had fallen to less than 40 percent. This change has had the effect of discouraging poor people from attending college, since they are much less willing (by almost 50 percent) to borrow money for education than are their wealthier counterparts (Mortenson, 1993, p. 21). Moreover, contemporary financial aid packages are far smaller than those of the past. For example, in 1993–1994 the maximum Pell grant was $2,300; in contrast, the G.I. Bill benefit would be more than $8,000 in 1993 dollars (National Commission on Responsibilities for Financing Postsecondary Education, 1993, p. 6).

Critics argue that the poor simply cannot afford to attend college with such low levels of support. Also, it is undeniable that financial aid has failed to keep pace with rising tuition levels. Between 1980 and 1990, college tuition and fees rose 126 percent, while the size of Pell grants rose only 37 percent (pp. 3, 4). The result is that higher education is becoming increasingly unaffordable for the poor.

Beyond these limitations, there are several weaknesses in current financial aid policy when judged according to the lessons learned in our study. As with colleges for the poor, financial aid is far more effective in helping disadvantaged students overcome the second barrier to higher education—getting into college—than the first—getting out of a poor neighborhood. As the Leslie and Brinkman study makes clear, hundreds of thousands of economically disadvantaged students attend college each year because of financial aid, and they would be unable to enroll without it. Even so, several flaws in the existing system loom large.

The most significant problem with financial aid as a central component of national policy for the poor is that it fails to incorporate most of the criteria deemed important in our study. Financial aid simply does not reach young kids. The original intention of the federal programs was to make student awards beginning in the ninth grade; however, annually changing funding levels, grant sizes, loan and grant mixes, and participation rates have made this impossible.

Because the federal financial aid program does not reach young children, it plays no part in their lives. Financial aid is therefore not linked with families and friends. It is not tied to the schools, where poor young people are not only economically disadvantaged but typically academically disadvantaged as well. They fall behind in grade level, take the wrong courses, and often drop out. It is a national, not a local, program, so it plays no role in the poor children's community, either. As a policy for helping poor children, financial aid has no relationship with building mentor teams for children or creating enrichment programs.

In short, financial aid does little to place a poor student at a college's doorstep; other programs identified in this study have to fulfill that role. However, it would be a mistake to assume that financial aid does not serve the poor. In fact, financial aid helps poor people walk through the college door and stay there until graduation. Although as college becomes more expensive, with all of its attendant logistical weaknesses and shrinking grant sizes, financial aid is becoming less effective at doing even this. And it does nothing to get at the basic problem that poor people do not see college as being for them.

Intervention Programs

We have noted that the primary weakness of both colleges for the poor and financial aid programs is their inability to help poor kids escape from the impoverished conditions in which they grow up. Yet our twenty-four–student study, as well as conversations with many poor kids and their families, indicate to us that the vast majority of poor young people can't even *imagine* going to college. By the time many poor kids are sixteen or seventeen years old, either they have already dropped out of school or they lag well behind their peers educationally. They fall victim to early pregnancy, drug and alcohol abuse, or the criminal justice system.

Reaching poor kids when they are still young often means approaching them while they are in school or even earlier. Since the Great Society days of the 1960s, a cornucopia of programs has been created to do exactly this. The past decade produced a further mushrooming of early intervention programs: school-based, family-based, community-based, peer-based—based in any social institution or organization that one can imagine.

The multiplicity of programs brought with them a multiplicity of goals, focusing on the range of causes and consequences of disadvantage. They employed an equally varied set of methods for achieving their goals. However, few of the initiatives have focused explicitly on college attendance as a goal. It is a truism though that any program designed to help kids successfully navigate growing up; staying away from drugs, gangs, or pregnancy; and getting through high school could be seen as providing many of the necessary precursors to a college education. However, we have chosen to examine three intervention programs that both target poor kids directly and emphasize college attendance as an explicit goal. These programs have been around for a while, some as long as four decades, and have therefore stood the tests of time and evaluation. In many ways they represent best efforts, despite what we identify as their students' limitations. They also employ three different strategies—differing in *how* and (especially important) *when* they enter a student's life.

Transition Programs

Transition programs attempt to bridge the gap between high school and college (or at whatever point a poor student is before coming to higher education). Nationally, the best-known of these programs—and the prototype for many of today's bridge programs—is Upward Bound.

A product of Lyndon Johnson's War on Poverty, Upward Bound was created by the Economic Opportunity Act of 1964 and was launched the following summer with joint funding from the federal government and the Carnegie Corporation. Its stated aim was to "break the cycle of poverty through higher education" by preparing low-income students with weak academic backgrounds or low educational aspirations for college (Schnitzer, 1989, p. 2).

Upward Bound is a campus-based initiative. Starting with seventeen pilot projects in 1965, the program quickly expanded to serve over 20,000 students at more than 200 colleges and universities in 1966. Collegiate participation has always been a competitive undertaking, with many more institutions applying for support than there are resources available to support. Colleges and universities are required to prepare proposals and apply for federal funding. Historically, priority has been given to programs targeted at inner-city school systems with large percentages of low-income students and high dropout rates. At least two-thirds of the students in each program must come from low-income backgrounds as well as be potential first-generation college students.

Every Upward Bound program is different. Working within federal guidelines, each institution plans its own program. Moreover, most programs do not begin until students are in the tenth or eleventh grade. In general, the programs start with an intensive six- or eight-week summer residential experience on a college or university campus. The original authorizing legislation mandated that students receive basic skills instruction in reading, writing, mathematics, and science. The 1976 reauthorization added personal, academic, and career counseling to the required list.

Over the years, numerous studies have attempted to gauge the effectiveness of Upward Bound. Unfortunately, the results of the studies have not been as useful as they might have been. Part of the problem is that much of the research has concentrated on single programs or on a small number of programs that tended to be more different than alike, given the decentralization of Upward Bound. In addition, the research has taken on the character of a cottage industry, with enormous variation in the methodologies employed.

However, several fairly comprehensive studies have been done. The most recent was conducted by the Research Triangle Institute (Burkheimer and Jaffe, 1982, p. 5). The initial phase of the study, in 1973–1974, came up with these major findings:

1. Upward Bound participants had substantially higher educational aspirations than did nonparticipants.

2. Upward Bound participants entered postsecondary education at a significantly higher rate than did nonparticipants; continuation rates for those in both groups who actually had entered college were about the same.

3. More Upward Bound students applied for financial aid than did comparable nonparticipants; while Upward Bound students received no more financial aid offers than did their counterparts, the aid they received was often packaged preferentially, with a higher percentage of grant than loan aid.

4. Minority students, poverty-level students, and students considered academic risks were more likely to enter higher education from Upward Bound projects than were nonparticipants.

5. Upward Bound students were more likely to attend four-year colleges than two-year postsecondary institutions.

6. No "systematic" differences in effectiveness were found across the varied types of projects when differences in the student populations were controlled.

The next phase of the study was conducted in 1978. The primary purpose of the follow-up was to "address questions concerning *long-term* progress, persistence, and performance in postsecondary education by former Upward Bound participants and comparable non-participants" (p. 10). The study further concluded:

1. Upward Bound was meeting its mandated objective of increasing the skills and aspirations requisite for entry into higher education.

2. It was less clear that Upward Bound provided the skills and motivation necessary for success in postsecondary education.

3. There was no evidence that Upward Bound participants had increased their academic skills in high school as indicated by grades. The study attributed this finding to the limited aca-

demic component of the program. The study found, however, that participation in the program increased survival skills—such as the ability to obtain more-adequate financial aid and a greater use of support services.

4. There was also no evidence that once enrolled in a postsecondary institution, Upward Bound participants performed better or had greater persistence than did nonparticipants. The authors of the study pointed out, however, that the program did not provide for any intervention once the student entered college.

The study concluded, "[I]t is strongly suggested that substantial numbers of former Upward Bound participants enter postsecondary education who would not have gone otherwise, and that a substantial percentage of these students will successfully complete a postsecondary program of study. Moreover, it is reasonable to assume that, as a result, these young people will obtain better jobs and, in general, lead more productive and satisfying lives" (p. 135).

The finding that Upward Bound has had a positive impact on college access is not surprising. The program applies many of the lessons we learned in our study. For one thing, it emphasizes enrichment activities. In many respects, Upward Bound telescopes or concentrates the years of supplemental activity prior to college that the students attending the selective university had experienced. The combination of activities is also very similar—additional course work, cultural exposure, social activity, support services, and finally, college courses—but Upward Bound provides it in a more organized, less individualized, and shorter-term fashion.

Upward Bound also offers the possibility of forming relationships with mentors and building mentor teams. The program attempts to build continuity in the relationships among students, teachers, and tutors. In the better Upward Bound programs, the same teaching staff goes through the program with the students, thereby providing sustained contact with a group of potential mentors. A limitation, however, is that such an arrangement does not generally include the group that has the largest impact on poor children–their immediate families.

While it is a strength that Upward Bound is rooted in precollege intervention, the program's timing does come into play a bit later than is optimally desirable. In theory, students can participate in Upward Bound as early as the hiatus between middle school and high school, but this is much more likely to occur after the sophomore or junior years of high school. Therefore, the program's focus is more on teenagers than on younger kids.

Upward Bound also reaches only a small segment of the people it could benefit—the best estimate is about one-fifth of the eligible population (Finifter, Baldwin, and Thelin, 1991, p. 170; Lowery, 1985, p. 11). The group it serves, however, is unlikely to be served elsewhere. Colleges for the poor, for example, tend to attract students who are highly motivated. In contrast, Upward Bound specifically targets those students with low aspirations who have historically been the least likely to attend college.

Transition programs do make a large contribution, particularly for poor young people. Yet they could be even more effective if they started earlier, lasted longer, reached out to the students' family members, and substantially enlarged the pool they served.

Early Intervention Programs

Early intervention programs are rooted in the belief that if poor people are to attend college, they need to be reached in childhood—that is, before they are irrevocably tracked away from college, can legally drop out of school, or make plans that preclude higher education.

A long-established example of an early intervention program is A Better Chance (ABC), which was discussed briefly in Chapter Two. Created in 1963 by a group of preparatory schools in the Northeast, ABC boomed between 1964 and 1975. During that decade, more than one hundred private schools—including a major-ity of the nation's most prestigious academies—participated in the program, as did a number of public schools that were added to the roster in the late 1960s.

Money flowed into the ABC coffers. After initial funding from the Rockefeller and Merrill foundations, the programs received nearly $5 million between 1965 and 1969 from the Office of Economic Opportunity (which was also supporting Upward Bound). The ABC program received substantial private funding as well, especially from corporations and foundations. Over time, however, the sources of ABC funding have shifted, and foundation support has dropped off, too. Only corporate assistance has risen.

The result is a lower funding base. Consequently, ABC has had to dramatically reduce its programming and cut back on recruitment and scholarships for low-income students. In 1984, the ABC board of trustees ended all supporting payments to participating schools, causing the program to lose much of its clout with these institutions. Today ABC, with a current budget of $1.6 million, involves more than 150 private and public schools. But the focus of ABC has shifted away from the poor and moved toward middle-class black students. The recruitment of low-income children from public schools gave way to middle-class black parents seeking out ABC for assistance in finding private schools for their children (Zweigenhaft and Domhoff, 1991, p. 8). ABC recruits and admits students "on the basis of academic merit, personal motivation, and promise" ("A Better Chance," 1993). It focuses on students who are in the top 10 percent of their class, have a grade average of at least 85 percent, and have good academic and personal recommendations; and on students from middle-class or poor but "stable" families ("A Better Chance," 1993; Mabry, 1991, p. 44).

Initially, the program had a residential orientation component for eight weeks in the summer; it was designed to give students a transitional experience and a chance to adjust to a very new and different lifestyle and culture. The summer orientation program provided the students with mentoring and consisted of intensive academic work, social and cultural activities, and athletic events—all with an accent on socialization. The orientation sought to instill middle-class manners and values. Even the dining room was used for this purpose (Zweigenhaft and Domhoff, p. 18). Now, with less revenue, the summer program is shorter.

The ABC program continues after the summer orientation. Once the students are enrolled, their progress in both social and academic situations is monitored by ABC staff and coordinators at the schools. ABC provides needed counseling and support to both students and their families, as well as information on additional educational opportunities, summer enrichment programs, and awards. The largest of the enrichment programs is the Leadership Education and Development program, which places minority students in summer programs at ten business schools across the country. Other summer programs provide enrichment or exploration opportunities in the liberal arts, the health professions, and international travel. In their junior and senior years of prep school, all ABC students are provided with information and contacts at colleges affiliated with the program.

Approximately 325 students are admitted to the ABC program each year; by June 30, 1991, more than 7,300 ABC students had graduated from prep schools. There are currently more than 1,100 students in the program. ABC does not publish attrition data, but by a very conservative estimate over 80 percent of matriculated ABC students graduate.

The ABC record is impressive. An early (1967) study of the program—done before ABC's focus shifted to middle-class children—compared forty-seven ABC participants with students that ABC was unable to place because of funding cuts. All of the ABC students went to college—many of them to Ivy League schools—while only 62 percent of the non-ABC students entered college (and only one attended an Ivy League school) (Zweigenhaft and Domhoff, p. 26). For black students in ABC, college participation rates of almost

100 percent stand in stark contrast to the rate for non-ABC black high school graduates, which hovers near 25 percent (Levine, A., 1989b).

Students in ABC not only go to college, they graduate. Consistently, over 90 percent of the program's students complete undergraduate degrees, with virtually all attending selective colleges and universities ("A Better Chance," 1993). A majority of ABC graduates report personal changes that they attribute specifically to the program, including more social awareness, independence, tolerance, academic competence, and awareness of the possibilities open to them (Zweigenhaft and Domhoff, pp. 65–66).

ABC's approach to getting poor people to attend college is very different from that of colleges for the poor or transition programs. ABC applies several of the strategies that make for an effective intervention effort. ABC places its emphasis on the first barrier that poor people face—getting out of poverty. In fact, although ABC offers college counseling and enrichment activities, it treats getting into higher education as almost an afterthought, almost as if college were simply the natural consequence of getting out of poverty via a boarding school.

Prior to its shift to a more middle-class focus, ABC had in place in varying degrees many of the lessons we learned from our study. It made use of accelerating institutions—the selective preparatory school. In addition, it intervened relatively early in the lives of poor children, sometimes as early as junior high school or the beginning of high school—not optimal but nevertheless a step in the right direction. It concentrated on identifying and training mentors from primary institutions—schools, churches, and youth organizations. It also involved the families of ABC students, although it fell short of emphasizing family support. It offered enrichment activities, including an orientation program designed to reduce the dissonance between the preparatory school and home environments. The continuation of ABC activities after the students had enrolled in prep schools was also an advance in design over the Upward Bound–like transition programs, which end at the time of matriculation.

Finally, the results of ABC were exceptional, before and after the shift. Nearly all of the students who completed preparatory school went on to college, and a very high percentage graduated. In addition, students generally attended the institutions of higher education that have historically been the least open to the poor— the nation's most selective colleges and universities.

There are limitations in ABC that merit attention. The first is its target population: the most talented young black people in the country. This is the group that Leslie and Brinkman (1988) found were most likely to attend college under any circumstances. The question then is whether most of these students would have gone to college even without ABC intervention. Based on current enrollment statistics, it is doubtful that they would have attended the elite colleges they did. To this extent, ABC may have been more useful in improving their position within higher education than it was in giving them access to college. It is important to question whether the ABC approach would work with less able and more academically disadvantaged youngsters.

The number of students served by ABC is very small—only 325 a year. Even with additional resources, could ABC ever be a mass program, enrolling tens of thousands of students? It seems unlikely, given the limited number of public and private prep schools in the United States.

The final issues are more theoretical than practical. ABC does not provide financial support for college. This has not been a serious problem for the program in recent years, given the types of students it selects and the schools they attend. Very able minority students enrolling in selective colleges and universities are likely to receive generous amounts of aid from both the government and the schools they attend. Under any other circumstances, however, this would be a critical concern.

A more pressing issue is one encountered by ABC student Edmund Perry at Exeter, whom we discussed in Chapter One. The program does about as much as possible to extricate poor children from poverty, but it cannot remove them totally. As a result, they are forced to live in two worlds—the elite preparatory school during the academic year and the poor neighborhood during vacations and visits home. The stress on these students is high, even though graduation rates seem at most minimally affected. Nonetheless, having to straddle the two worlds highlights the need for parent education to support students when they come home. It also speaks to the value of summer enrichment activities away from highly dysfunctional home environments; the Milton Hershey School in Pennsylvania, for example, has found such activities very helpful to their low-income residential population.

By moving beyond the transition programs and reaching children younger than do either the colleges for the poor or financial aid programs, ABC has proved that if applying the lessons we recommend based on our study is an asset even with the best and brightest young people, it is obviously crucial for other kids with fewer advantages.

Comprehensive Programs

Perhaps today's most talked about program for increasing college access for the poor is one that employs more of the lessons from our study than anything else we have observed. It reaches kids when they are young, provides enrichment activities, builds mentor teams, thinks locally, and plans individually. It also has the potential of large-scale replication while remaining local, and it offers financial aid. And it began quite by accident.

In June 1981, Eugene Lang was asked to deliver a graduation speech to fifty-four members of the sixth-grade class at P.S. 121, a school he had attended fifty-three years earlier. Lang, the son of immigrants, had grown up in the East Harlem section of New York City where P.S. 121 is located. He had completed high school in the area, and then took a job as a dishwasher at a restaurant in the city. One night, while Lang was filling in for a sick waiter, a frequent patron of the restaurant asked him why he had not attended college. Lang answered that his parents, only recently arrived in the United States, were unable to afford it. Several nights later, the patron returned with a catalog from Swarthmore College and urged Lang to apply. The patron helped Lang prepare an application and arranged an interview with Swarthmore's dean. Lang was admitted to the college on a scholarship and went on to earn a bachelor's degree. After college, he followed a career in business, founding and serving as president of REFAC Corporation, a company that transforms new technologies into commercial ventures. Lang believed that his career and financial success had been made possible only because of the opportunities college had afforded him.

As he was about to make his speech at P.S. 121, Lang observed his audience. He noted that the student body had changed dramatically since he graduated. It was now predominantly black and Hispanic, rather than white and ethnic as in his day. But it was still largely made up of children from poor families; many of the parents were recent immigrants to the United States. Lang discarded his prepared text and instead made a spontaneous promise to the children.

"This is your first graduation—the time to dream," he said. "Dream about your future—what you want to be. Believe in that dream and be prepared to work for it. And that means staying in school and learning. . . . Always remember, your dream is important—and education is the key to the future. Don't think for a minute that you can't go to college. You can! I repeat, you *can* go to college—because right now, to each of you, I make this promise: when you graduate from junior high school, I will give each of you a scholarship of $500 a year for your college tuition. More than that, if you stay in school through high school, I will increase that scholarship each year so that, when you receive your high school diploma and are ready for college, *you will be able to go*" (Richmond, 1990, pp. 227–229).

Lang's offhanded promise evolved into a comprehensive college-access program that added the elements of tutoring, counseling, and support to the offer of money. Lang ultimately agreed to pay the difference between the cost of attending the colleges to which the students were accepted and any federal, state, or institutional aid received by the students—thus providing early assurance that if they were accepted to college, the full cost would be covered. Lang calculated that an investment of $200,000 with accrued interest would sufficiently cover the total amount required by the students at P.S. 121. His estimate was low.

But it soon became apparent to Lang that financial aid was not enough. College was too many years away; the students were only halfway through the schooling they needed to get to higher education. Large obstacles already existed—academic, social, personal, and economic—that would diminish the chances that the students would ever complete school. P.S. 121 was among the lowest-ranked elementary schools in New York City in terms of academic performance. In the six years that lay ahead of them prior to college, Lang's sixth-graders faced obstacles that would only grow larger and more formidable.

In response to these threats, Lang rented space in a neighborhood house to provide services to the children—whom he called dreamers—and their families. He offered counseling, tutoring, mentoring, and enrichment activities that included group trips, summer jobs, social services, and guest visitors. Lang's center also served as a bunker—a safe place for the dreamers to gather, stay in touch, and talk—particularly as they grew older and fanned out to high schools across New York City. Lang hired a young neighborhood social-service worker named Johnny Rivera to coordinate all of the activities. Lang and Rivera worked together with the children and their families through their junior high, senior high, and college years.

Contact was close and personal between the adults and the dreamers: Lang often invited the students to meet with him individually at his office to discuss their progress and to provide whatever intervention was necessary to keep them going.

The results of Lang's efforts were astounding. Ten years after he first made his promise, 90 percent of the P.S. 121 sixth-graders had graduated from high school or obtained a GED degree. (The original estimate, based on prior history, was that at least 75 percent of the students would drop out of school.) After high school, 50 percent of the students went on to postsecondary education; the best estimate is that over 70 percent will complete at least two years of postsecondary education. (The original projection was that none would attend college [I Have A Dream Foundation brochure, New York, 1993]).

The results have not been uniform. Students have dropped out of school, and youngsters have moved and left the program. At least one student went to prison for armed robbery; Lang encouraged him to study for a GED while incarcerated. After the student's release from prison, Lang arranged a job for him at a hospital and enrolled him at La Guardia Community College in a night program for a paramedical license. Unfortunately, that dreamer committed another crime and returned to prison (Coons and Petrick, 1992, p. 86).

Eugene Lang's program received a great deal of national media attention. As a result, he was inundated with requests from people around the country for help in establishing programs like his. In response, Lang created the I Have A Dream Foundation (IHAD) to encourage and support programs like that at P.S. 121. Today, there are more than 140 programs in more than forty cities in over half the states in the country; together, they serve more than 10,000 dreamers.

IHAD has codified the elements of the original program into five guidelines for the creation of new I Have A Dream projects. First, there must be a sponsor—an individual or a small group of people—willing to adopt an entire elementary school class and devote the time necessary to develop relationships with the children. Second, the sponsor must make a commitment of at least $350,000. The money can come from a single individual or be raised from the community—individuals, corporations, foundations, churches, civic groups, fund-raising events, and the like. Third, the sponsor, with assistance from the local school, must identify an elementary school class; IHAD suggests that the fourth, fifth, and sixth grades be targeted—the recommendation is the earlier the better. Fourth, the sponsor must hire a full-time program coordinator—a counseling professional experienced in working with children—who will be involved daily with the students, their families, and their schools. Volunteers and mentors must also be recruited to work with the dreamers. Finally, the sponsor must obtain a physical location to serve as an activity base for the program coordinator and the students; it can be at a community service facility, a school, or a college. With assistance from IHAD, the sponsor and program coordinator must develop a program that includes academic, cultural, and support activities. IHAD assists its new projects with staff support and guidance as useful to each particular site. (I Have A Dream Foundation brochure, 1993, pp. 12–13).

The resulting IHAD projects have not by any means taken on a cookie-cutter sameness. Some very interesting experiments have been attempted. For example, some projects have been initiated earlier than recommended: IHAD programs have been created for third-graders in Pasadena, California, and in Chicago. And several of the efforts have not focused exclusively on access to college. Recognizing that higher education is not appropriate for all young people, a number of new IHAD projects now include post–high school vocational education and even job placement.

The IHAD sponsors have not all been philanthropists and business people like Eugene Lang. For instance, Grinnell College has been a sponsor working with 100 students in nearby Des Moines, Iowa. Churches and synagogues in New York, Illinois, Connecticut, and Texas have created programs, too. Perhaps the most dramatic variation is in Boca Raton, Florida: the target is not a school but the fourth- through ninth-graders who live in a housing project and attend several different elementary schools (Coons and Petrick, pp. 89–92).

In terms of the lessons from our twenty-four–student study, the I Have A Dream program hits all the bases for young people. It touches kids early, reaching them in elementary school, generally between the ages of nine and twelve. It is a local program, tailored to the community. And it includes a planned program of academic and social enrichment activities, as well as support services. In a number of the IHAD projects, these activities have been tailored to the individual needs of dreamers. For example, in one project a sponsor arranged for two students who wanted to become pilots to visit an airport, talk with a commercial pilot, and receive flight lessons. In another case, a student with an interest in medicine got to visit with a surgeon and observe an operation. Similarly, a student excited by cosmetology was given a chance to manage a beauty parlor (p. 85).

Another ingredient in the IHAD program is its focus on the critical primary institutions in the students' lives—their families, schools, and community organizations. This helps foster mentoring teams by increasing the probability that children will receive needed attention from adults in two or more areas of their lives. Finally, IHAD offers guaranteed financial support for college, opening every sector of higher education to the dreamers—even those historically deemed least available to the poor. IHAD places influential people at the center of the program in the positions of sponsor and program coordinator. Their jobs encompass those specific activities that characterize the mentors in our study—imparting hope, building confidence, stressing the importance of education, and bringing students to the college gate.

The IHAD program is different from the other strategies for increasing college access for the poor. More than any of the other programs, IHAD is balanced in its focus on the twin obstacles facing poor students. It seeks to help students break out of poverty by intervening early in their lives, preferably before they fall victim to their neighborhoods; it aims to enlarge the vision of the future life possibilities for dreamers; and it attempts to build understanding and support for the dreamers' future choices by working with their families, schools, and local communities. At the same time, IHAD tries to help students overcome the barriers to college access. It does this by guaranteeing college tuition, strengthening academic skills, and building students' knowledge of and aspirations for higher education.

The notion of guaranteed college tuition is unique. To some degree, such a guarantee was the hope for the initial federal financial aid programs. The intent was to let children and their families know in elementary school that money would be available for their higher education; families would pay no more for college than they could afford. However, the reality is that funding levels for the government programs have never been high enough or consistent enough to make either the guarantee or the affordability a reality. Berea College has also attempted to achieve the same goals as IHAD. While it is able to offer free tuition, the students must still pay for room, board, and the extras. The college's labor program helps, as does financial aid, but the result is not a guarantee of a college education.

In this sense, IHAD is the only college access program that opens up every sector of higher education to poor people. While all of the other strategies enhance access—they get students into college—ABC gets them into some of the most selective colleges in the country. What is significant is that I Have A Dream is the only strategy that goes beyond access to choice. It permits students to attend any college that will admit them, without worrying about the cost. In this way, very able but poor students are not restricted to attending low-cost, open-admission community colleges; they can actually enroll in an expensive selective residential college without having to consider its cost.

In this regard, IHAD not only gives the poor a chance at the whole world of higher education to the poor—it also opens every sector of higher education to the full spectrum of poor young people. IHAD is the least selective of the strategies we examined. ABC, for example, seeks the best and the brightest; Upward Bound aims to serve the underprepared and those with low educational aspirations; and federal financial aid programs and institutions like Hostos Community College are open to all poor people. However, those programs begin too late to reach many poor students. By the time the programs are realities, many students are too far off the college track to benefit from them. I Have A Dream, by contract, reaches the students when they are still in elementary school. It is an inclusive program that embraces a whole class of students from the most able to the least, from those with the highest educational aspirations to those with the lowest.

What makes it possible for IHAD to serve such a wide range of abilities and backgrounds is another unique feature of the program—it is small and can be individualized. The typical project serves fewer than 100 students; it has a full-time program coordinator, one or more people serving as sponsors, and usually a group of volunteers who work with these students. The small size and individual staffing enables IHAD to arrange activities such as the visits to the airport, the operating room, and the beauty salon. They make it possible for a special program to be created for a dreamer in prison. In their study of the IHAD program, Christopher Coons and Elizabeth Petrick tell an anecdote that drives home the point. The mother of an IHAD student in Chicago died, leaving the dreamer and her brother as orphans. The children were to become wards of the state. The IHAD sponsor paid for the mother's funeral, served as a pallbearer, and located a woman who had once lived in the children's housing project to become their guardian. The program coordinator and a tutor also attended the funeral. The program coordinator then helped the children through the legal-guardianship process and assisted them in moving into their new home (Coons and Petrick, p. 85).

Hand in hand with the individualization comes an almost opposite virtue: IHAD is capable of mass production. The program can be replicated in any location in the country and adapted to the specific circumstances of the community. Only Upward Bound approaches IHAD in this combination of characteristics, but Upward Bound has not been historically as individualized a program.

Part of the explanation for the differences between Upward Bound and I Have A Dream is time. Of all the strategies discussed, IHAD is the most intensive. Not only does it begin the earliest in students' lives, but it lasts the longest and has the greatest potential continuity. IHAD is at least a ten-year intervention—three years of junior high school, three years of high school, and four years of college; it can be even longer if the program starts in fourth grade. Also, it can include every aspect of a child's life—home, school, friends, and community. This comprehensiveness and sustained activity is unique to I Have A Dream—it is a long-term developmental strategy.

However, it would be a mistake to regard IHAD as a panacea. Like the other access strategies we discussed, IHAD has weaknesses. For one, it is a small program—while it can be re-created endlessly, at the moment it touches only 10,000 students. It can't compare in size to, for example, the federal financial aid programs. IHAD is also random: which classes of young people it selects and what cities they live in is entirely serendipitous and at the whim of the sponsors.

The net for the program may be too wide, as well. IHAD is as likely to involve students for whom college is not the best choice after high school as those for whom it is. There is no selectivity or screening.

The IHAD programs also vary in quality. Some elements work better than others. Lack of effective parental involvement, for example, has been a shortcoming in many of the projects. Moreover, some programs are better organized than others. In addition, some programs have not endured. One sponsor withdrew from the program after pledging to send a class to college and two other sponsors died, leaving the children sponsorless and therefore without a program. However, the largest issue may be the lack of understanding of what makes IHAD effective. There is no research base to indicate which elements of the program work and which do not. Our study points to some potential reasons why some elements work, but more research is needed. New IHAD programs follow a rather ritualistic formula: they incorporate all guidelines suggested by the foundation. By so doing, the salubrious elements are indistinguishable from the others. The efficacy and need for each of the activities that make up the program is untested.

All of this said, I Have A Dream is one of the most effective programs ever attempted for increasing access to college by the poor. It shows just how powerful comprehensive programs can be if they incorporate the full range of lessons that the twenty-four poor students in our study taught us. National education policy that incorporates the lessons of IHAD can have a profound impact on increasing access to higher education for poor Americans.

For more than 350 years, our country has experimented with a plethora of approaches to making college a reality for poor people. During the past half century, based on these experiments, the United States has lurched toward a national policy for achieving this end. We are convinced that America today has the knowledge and the experience to take the final step. All we need is the will to do so.

Appendix A

Brief Biographies of the Twenty-Four Students Interviewed

This book tells the stories of twenty-four students. In the preceding pages, these students' lives were dissected and used as anecdotes or illustrations. Here, we offer a picture of each of the people who were kind enough to participate in this study, as they were at the time interviewed them.

Community College Students Interviewed

Barry is a white male, age thirty-eight, who grew up in Providence, Rhode Island, as one of eight children in a female-headed family. Neither of his parents had attended college. He started using drugs in high school and dropped out in tenth grade. Fed up with both his family and school, Barry left home at age sixteen, got his own apartment, and started working for a moving company. He worked as a mover for twenty years, but a ruptured disk made it impossible to remain in that line of work. Surgery, physical rehabilitation, vocational counseling, and finally college followed his injury. Barry is now divorced and has an eleven-year-old daughter. He will be graduating from the two-year college as this book goes to print.

Billy is a twenty-seven-year-old single white male from Lawrence, Massachusetts. He is the middle child among five siblings. His father was an alcoholic who taught Billy to drink in grade school. Billy dropped out of school three times and never completed high school; his parents showed no concern. He was using drugs and alcohol seriously by the end of eighth grade. (His oldest brother followed the same pattern and is now in prison for bank robbery.) Billy spent a couple of years neither in school nor working—just drinking and doing drugs. When his life seemed to be careening out of control, Billy decided to join the navy. Although he earned a GED while serving, he was later discharged following repeated bouts with drugs and alcohol and being absent without leave. When Billy returned home, he began seeing a therapist. He is now just a few courses short of completing an associate degree at the community college.

Dawn is a twenty-nine-year-old divorced white female with two children. She was born in Cranston, Rhode Island, one of thirteen children. After her mother divorced Dawn's alcoholic father, Dawn and her siblings were placed in foster care when she was eleven. The children, who were put into separate homes in groups of two or three, moved frequently. Dawn did poorly in school and was held back twice. She dropped out after giving birth to her first child in tenth grade; another baby followed three years later, and Dawn married the father. Two years after the second child was born, with her husband out of work, Dawn worked two or three low-level service jobs at a time. The marriage ended in divorce when Dawn was only twenty-three. She took her two children and was homeless for five months. After several undesirable housing placements by social service agencies, Dawn and her children moved into an apartment in a public housing project. She entered counseling and was steered to completing a GED. The housing department staff encouraged her to attend college. Today, Dawn is in her third year at the community college as a part-time student.

Debbie is a twenty-nine-year-old divorced white mother of two from Providence, Rhode Island. Her parents, neither of whom had completed secondary schools, divorced when she was nine years old. Debbie, her mother, and her three siblings were forced to move in with her grandmother. Her father did not pay child support, so Debbie's mother had to take a full-time job at night. Debbie became a mother of sorts to her siblings, and communication between mother and daughter broke down. Debbie did poorly in school; she joined the army immediately after high school. There she met her husband, a career officer from an affluent East Coast family. The marriage ended in divorce, and the event shattered Debbie's self-esteem. She returned to her mother's home with her children and signed up for public assistance. Debbie is now in her third year as a student at the community college.

Francois is a thirty-nine-year old divorced black male from the Dominican Republic. He grew up in a large, extended farm family with two siblings. Neither of his parents had much formal education. His father died when Francois was twelve. Francois attended a Jesuit school until the age of thirteen, when he was expelled for disrupting class; after that, he completed public schooling. Following graduation from high school, he came to the United States to join his mother, who had immigrated several years earlier. A series of jobs followed, along with an occasional college course. Francois has twin three-year-old sons; it was for the sake of his children, he said, that he enrolled in college. Francois is a second-year community college student.

Fred is a single white male, age twenty-three, from Quincy, Massachusetts. He is the oldest of five children from a broken family that moved frequently. Fred was forced to serve as a surrogate father to his brothers and sisters. He was identified as a gifted child early in elementary school. By ninth grade, however, Fred was chronically tardy and truant, had been suspended from school, and was failing classes. He dropped out of high school. Within two years of leaving school, under pressure from his mother, Fred earned a GED and enrolled in college. He is now a second-year student at the community college.

Lela is a twenty-nine-year-old female Iranian immigrant who has been in the country for three and a half years. She lives in a housing project with her husband, two children, mother, and aunt.

Lela was adopted as an infant by a sixty-five-year-old Iranian man and his thirty-five-year-old wife. The wife, who resented Lela, had agreed to the adoption only because of the dowry possibilities. When Lela was nine, her mother began pushing her to get married. To escape her mother after her father's death, Lela married when she was nineteen. After the Islamic revolution, when it became difficult for a Christian family like Lela's to live in Iran, she and her extended family escaped to Germany, where they lived in a refugee camp. Two years later, Lela and her family managed to immigrate to the United States with assistance from a human-services agency. She enrolled in the community college right after arriving in the United States.

Leo is a single black twenty-two-year-old native of the Canary Islands. Wheelchair-bound and almost totally unable to speak due to polio contracted when he was seven, Leo communicates by laptop computer. He resided in Cape Verde with his grandmother, aunt, and uncle, then came to the United States at the age of twelve to live with his father, stepmother, and four stepsiblings in Providence, Rhode Island. The family, always in need of money, moved after Leo graduated from high school. He took a year off from school prior to enrolling in college. Today, he is a fourth-year student at the community college.

Lori is a single twenty-year-old white female from the South Shore of Massachusetts. She grew up in a physically and verbally abusive family, and her father was an alcoholic. After her parents divorced when she was four, Lori lived with her mother and two siblings. Lori had a "stormy" relationship with her mother. She was counseled for depression and had a poor school record because of truancy. She graduated from a vocational high school and took a job as a cosmetologist. After two years working in a salon, she became bored and enrolled in the community college, where she is now a second-year student.

Meredith is a thirty-nine-year-old single white female. She grew up in New Haven, Connecticut, with her parents and a younger sibling. Although her family was relatively well-to-do, Meredith got involved with drugs and has consequently lived in poverty much of her life. She hit the streets "after the ninth grade," becoming an alcoholic and a heroin user. Since she left her family, Meredith's life has included several near-fatal drug overdoses; at least one suicide attempt; arrests for writing bad checks, embezzlement, and fighting; and many jobs primarily in the service sector. After an overdose when she was thirty-five, Meredith sought treatment and counseling. She has been sober for more than three years, although her companion is a heavy drinker. Meredith, who lives on welfare and disability insurance, is completing a degree at the community college.

Nordim is a single twenty-six-year-old male refugee from a small village in Cambodia. He is the youngest of eight children. His mother came from a poor farming family, and his father, from a more urban background, was not formally educated either. When Nordim was nine, his father was taken away by the Khmer Rouge and was never seen or heard from again. A year later, Nordim and his family were evacuated from their village and resettled by the Khmer Rouge, but in separate locations. Only he and his mother were allowed to maintain contact with each other, albeit from separate villages. He was subsequently placed in a relocation camp. Only one brother and one sister survived the ordeal. In 1984, Nordim managed to escape to the Thai border, then spent the next three and a half years in a refugee camp, where he learned some English and French and found work as a laborer. When he was twenty-three, Nordim immigrated to the United States and settled near Providence, Rhode Island, where he had relatives. His aunt made arrangements for him to take English as a Second Language courses and enroll in college. He is currently a third-year student at the community college.

Peggy is a thirty-one-year-old divorced white mother of two living on welfare. She grew up in cities around Providence, Rhode Island. When her parents divorced and her mother remarried, she and her brother were adopted by their stepfather. Money was very limited, and food was in short supply. After Peggy graduated from high school, she married a man who was in the air force. When the marriage ended four years later, Peggy returned to her mother's home, where she lived in the attic, went into a deep depression, and entered therapy. Peggy then enrolled in college, and today she is a third-year student.

Selective University Students Interviewed

Anita is a twenty-year-old single white female from Boston. She is an only child of parents who had not completed high school. After her father died when Anita was three, her mother moved with her to Florida and worked as a waitress there. When Anita was nine, they returned to Boston, where they lived with Anita's grandmother in a small one-bedroom apartment. Anita attended Catholic school and was identified as an academic achiever. Anita's mother, who was supportive of her daughter's education—though not committed to it—died while Anita was in high school. Anita moved in with an aunt in the Boston suburbs and continued to attend the same Boston high school. She is now a junior at the selective university.

Brenda is a twenty-one-year-old single black woman from Chicago. She grew up in a family consisting of her mother, stepfather, and younger stepsister. Brenda was identified early in life as a precocious child. As a result, she received a large scholarship and was admitted in fifth grade to one of Chicago's most selective schools. Things fell apart for Brenda four years later: her parents divorced, her mother didn't want her, and Brenda and her sisters went to live with her stepfather and his new wife. Her stepfather refused to send her back to the private school, insisting she enroll in a public high school. Tension in the family was high, and Brenda was very unhappy. Her debate coach from the private school invited Brenda to live with her and return to the school; Brenda's stepfather readily agreed. Except for a summer at Phillips Andover Academy, she stayed with the debate coach and her family until she graduated from high school. Today, Brenda is a junior at the selective university.

Chris is a twenty-year-old single Hispanic male. His grandparents, who never went beyond junior high school, worked as migrant laborers along with their children. To escape a life working in the strawberry fields, Chris's father joined the military. Chris's father completed high school; he does not know whether his mother did or not. His family moved often. Chris was born in Georgia, then lived in California, spent several years in the Philippines, returned to California, moved to Germany, and settled in New Mexico. Chris, who is the oldest child in his family, has three siblings. The first member of his extended family ever to attend college, Chris is now a junior at the selective university.

Damon is a nineteen-year-old black male from New York City's Harlem. His parents came north from Mississippi, where their families had long worked in the fields. His mother died when he was eight. The youngest of three siblings, he was a bright youngster whose parents believed strongly in education and had enrolled him in private schools from the start. He attended one of the most prestigious preparatory schools in New York City, on Manhattan's Upper East Side. Damon is currently a sophomore at the selective university.

James is a single Mexican American male, age nineteen, from California's Central Valley. He is the middle child of a very close family of seven deeply religious fundamentalist Protestants. As resources are few, they regularly pray for rent money and food. Neither of James's parents had formal schooling beyond high school. James attended a number of different schools—Catholic, Protestant, secular, private, and public. He was a good student and athlete, and his parents told him that he could be anything he wanted to be. James is now a sophomore at the selective university.

Jenny is an eighteen-year-old single white female from North Dakota. She is the oldest of ten children. Her parents are Protestant fundamentalists, and Jenny's family lived a hand-to-mouth existence at a religious retreat center. She was home-schooled through tenth grade, when she wrote the State of North Dakota complaining about the quality of her education. Attendance at a religious academy and a public school followed. Although Jenny's parents urged her to marry rather than attend college, she is currently a freshman at the selective university.

Juan is an eighteen-year-old single Mexican American male from Texas. He was born in Mexico to parents who had less than an elementary school education. Juan is the oldest male among six siblings. When he was ten years old, Juan and his father entered the United States illegally to find work. They stayed with an uncle, who without asking permission simply enrolled his nephew in school, which Juan had not been attending in Mexico. After two years, Juan and his father returned to Mexico. There Juan worked in construction until a poor economy brought him back to the United States. Once again, the uncle put Juan in school. Juan was fourteen years old. Despite initial language difficulties, Juan was identified as a high-ability student at the Catholic middle school he was attending. He passed the entrance exam and went on to graduate from one of the most competitive secondary schools in San Antonio. Today, he is a freshman at the selective university.

Juanita is a twenty-one-year-old single Chicana from southern Texas. She grew up with a single mother who had immigrated from Mexico. Her mother had serious heart problems and little education. Juanita, who had one younger sister, was identified by her public grade-school teachers as a high-ability student. The teachers developed enrichment programs for Juanita and also monitored her dating and extracurricular life. After her mother suffered a serious heart attack when Juanita was sixteen, she attempted to drop out of school to support her family, but the school counseling staff refused to let her. Juanita was the valedictorian of her graduating class and is now a senior at the selective university.

Lester is a single eighteen-year-old white male from Maine. He grew up in a farm family, including a father and mother who hadn't attended college and an older sister who had. Money is tight in Lester's family. His father wanted Lester to attend a local college and return afterward to his community and the family farm, which is doing very poorly; Lester's teachers concurred. His older sister told him to apply to a selective university and plan for a different kind of future. Lester is currently a freshman at the selective university.

Lin is a single twenty-year-old Asian female from Detroit. She was born in Vietnam and came to the United States at the age of four. Her parents operate a small grocery store in the inner city. Their hours are long and they have a difficult time making ends meet. Lin attended a neighborhood elementary school and a magnet high school specializing in music. Her grades and test scores were so outstanding that she spent a summer during high school attending classes at Stanford University, where her older sister was a student. While growing up, Lin alternated her spare time between studying, tagging after her older sister, and being with a few close college-bound friends. For Lin's parents, preparing their children to attend a "good" college was a top priority. Today, Lin is a junior at the selective university.

Maria is a nineteen-year-old single Hispanic female from Florida. An only child, she does not know who her father is. She was raised by her mother, a Colombian immigrant who never completed elementary school and does not speak English. Maria was an outstanding student—one of the best in her class throughout primary and secondary school in Miami. Her mother is a true believer in education who desperately wants a better life for her daughter. The night before she was to have surgery, Maria's mother made her promise to attend one of the Ivy League universities to which she had been admitted—despite opposition from her extended family in Colombia, who wanted Maria to remain with her mother. Maria is now a sophomore at the selective university.

Sarah is a twenty-year-old single female from the South Bronx in New York City. Her parents, a black woman and a Jewish man, are divorced. Sarah lived first with her mother and then with her father, an unemployed craftsman who never completed high school. The family moved several times before the divorce, and Sarah attended a number of neighborhood schools in the area. She passed the entrance exam and went on to graduate from the highly selective Bronx High School of Science. Her home situation was tense, and Sarah often clashed with her stepmother and stepsister. For her father, education is a top priority. Sarah is currently a junior at the selective university.

. . . .

Comparative Statistics*

Table B.1. Institutions Attended by Students.

Community college	(12) 50 percent
Selective university	(12) 50 percent

Table B.2. Gender of Students Interviewed.

	Community college	Selective university	Total
Male	(6) 50 percent	(6) 50 percent	(12) 50 percent
Female	(6) 50 percent	(6) 50 percent	(12) 50 percent

Table B.3. Racial/Ethnic Background of Students Interviewed.

	Community college	Selective university	Total
White	(9) 75 percent	(3) 25 percent	(12) 50 percent
Black	(2) 17 percent	(2) 17 percent	(4) 17 percent
Interracial		(1) 8 percent	(1) 4 percent
Hispanic		(5) 42 percent	(5) 21 percent
Asian	(1) 8 percent	(1) 8 percent	(2) 8 percent

*Numbers may not add up to 100 percent due to rounding errors.

Table B.4. Ages of Students Interviewed.

Age	Community college	Selective university	Total
18		(3) 25 percent	(3) 13 percent
19		(3) 25 percent	(3) 13 percent
20	(1) 8 percent	(5) 42 percent	(6) 25 percent
21		(1) 8 percent	(1) 4 percent
22	(1) 8 percent		(1) 4 percent
23	(1) 8 percent		(1) 4 percent
24			
25			
26	(1) 8 percent		(1) 4 percent
27	(1) 8 percent		(1) 4 percent
28			
29	(3) 25 percent		(3) 13 percent
30			
31	(1) 8 percent		(1) 4 percent
32			
33			
34			
35			
36			
37			
38	(1) 8 percent		(1) 4 percent
39	(2) 17 percent		(2) 8 percent

Table B.5. Region Where Students Interviewed Grew Up.

	Community college	Selective university	Total
West		(5) 42 percent	(5) 21 percent
Midwest		(2) 17 percent	(2) 8 percent
South		(1) 8 percent	(1) 4 percent
New England	(8) 68 percent	(2) 17 percent	(10) 42 percent
Middle Atlantic States		(2) 17 percent	(2) 8 percent
Abroad	(4) 33 percent		(4) 17 percent

Table B.6. Family Background of Students Interviewed.

	Community college	Selective university	Total
Grew up with one or no parent at home	(9) 75 percent	(6) 50 percent	(15) 63 percent
Grew up with two parents at home	(3) 25 percent	(6) 50 percent	(9) 38 percent

Table B.7. Attendance at Preparatory Schools by Students Interviewed.

	Community college	Selective university	Total
Attended preparatory or selective public school		(6) 50 percent	(6) 25 percent
Did not attend preparatory or selective public school	(12) 100 percent	(6) 50 percent	(18) 75 percent

Table B.8. School Completion by Students Interviewed.

	Community college	Selective university	Total
Dropped out of school	(6) 50 percent		(6) 25 percent
Did not drop out of school	(6) 50 percent	(12) 100 percent	(18) 75 percent

Table B.9. Precipitating Event Experienced Prior to Enrolling in College for Students Interviewed.

	Community college	Selective university	Total
Immigration	(4) 33 percent		(4) 17 percent
Divorce	(3) 25 percent		(3) 13 percent
Illness	(3) 25 percent		(3) 13 percent
None	(2) 17 percent	(12) 100 percent	(14) 58 percent

Table B.10. Mentors of Students Interviewed.

	Community college	Selective university	Total
Mother	(1) 8 percent	(2) 17 percent	(3) 13 percent
Father		(2) 17 percent	(2) 8 percent
Both parents		(1) 8 percent	(1) 4 percent
Other family members	(1) 8 percent	(3) 25 percent	(4) 17 percent
Teacher		(2) 17 percent	(2) 8 percent
Coach		(1) 8 percent	(1) 4 percent
Guidance counselor	(1) 8 percent		(1) 4 percent
Vocational counselor	(1) 8 percent		(1) 4 percent
Therapist	(3) 25 percent		(3) 13 percent
Human-services officer	(3) 25 percent		(3) 13 percent
Neighbor	(1) 8 percent		(1) 4 percent
None	(1) 8 percent	(1) 8 percent	(2) 8 percent

References

Alger, H., Jr. *Ragged Dick*. New York: Collier Books, 1962. (Originally published 1868.)

Allmendinger, D. *Paupers and Scholars*. New York: St. Martin's Press, 1975.

Alterman, R. C. *Manpower Policy and Individual Need in the Development of Federal Aid to College Students*. Social Foundation of Education Monograph Series. Ann Arbor: School of Education, University of Michigan, 1973.

Anderson, J. "The Hampton Model of Normal School and Industrial Education, 1868–1900," in V. P. Franklin and J. Anderson (eds.), *New Perspectives on Black Educational History*. Boston: G. K. Hall, 1978.

Anson, R. S. *Best Intentions: The Education and Killing of Edmund Perry*. New York: Vantage Books, 1987.

Astin, A. *Achieving Educational Excellence*. San Francisco: Jossey-Bass, 1985.

Bethune, M. M. "How Bethune-Cookman College Campus Started." In L. Kerber, and J. De Hart-Mathews (eds.), *Women's America: Refocusing the Past*. New York: Oxford University Press, 1987.

Breed, M. B. "The Private Boarding-House for College Women," *Religious Education*, April 4, 1909, 60–64.

Brint, S., and Karabel, J. *The Diverted Dream: Community Colleges and the Promise of Educational Opportunities in America 1900–1975*. New York: Oxford University Press, 1989.

Brown, C. *Manchild in the Promised Land*. New York: Macmillan, 1966.

Burkheimer, G. J., and Jaffe, J. "Highly Able Students Who Did Not Go to College." Washington, D.C.: National Center for Education Statistics, 1982.

Butterfield, F. "Programs Seek to Stop Trouble Before It Starts." *New York Times*, December 30, 1994, A11.

Carey, J. C. *Kansas State University: The Quest for Identity*. Lawrence: The Regents Press of Kansas, 1977.

Chickering, A. *Commuting Versus Resident Students: Overcoming the Educational Inequities of Living Off Campus*. San Francisco: Jossey-Bass, 1974.

Chronicle of Higher Education Almanac, 61(1), September 1994, 5–119.

Clark, B. *The Open Door College: A Case Study*. New York: McGraw-Hill, 1960.

Clifford, G. J., and Guthrie, J. *Ed School*. Chicago: University of Chicago Press, 1988.

Cohen, A., and Brawer, F. B. *The American Community College*. San Francisco: Jossey-Bass, 1982.

Coons, C. A., and Petrick, E. W. "A Decade of Making Dreams into Reality: Lessons from the I Have A Dream Program." *Yale Law and Policy Review*, 1992, 10(1), 82–103.

Curti, M., and Carstensen, V. *The University of Wisconsin: A History, Volumes I and II*. Madison: University of Wisconsin Press, 1949.

Davis, J. S., and Johns, K., Jr. "Change in Low Income Freshmen Participation in College 1966 to 1986." *Journal of Student Financial Aid*, 1989, 19(1), 56–62.

Dixon, R., "Parents of Illinois Eighth Graders: A Survey of Their Knowledge About Academic and Financial Planning for Their Child's Education Beyond High School." *Journal of Student Financial Aid*, 1988, 19(1), 29–36.

Dwork, D. *Children with a Star: Jewish Youth in Nazi Europe*. New Haven, Conn.: Yale University Press, 1991.

Evans, T. W. *Mentors: Making a Difference in Our Public Schools*. Princeton, N. J.: Peterson's Guides, 1992.

Finifter, D. H., Baldwin, R. G., and Thelin, J. R. *The Uneasy Public Policy Triangle in Higher Education: Quality, Diversity, and Budgetary Efficiency*. New York: ACE/Oryx, 1991.

Geiger, L. G. *University of the Northern Plains: A History of the University of North Dakota, 1883–1958*. Grand Forks: University of North Dakota Press, 1958.

Gray, J. *The University of Minnesota, 1851–1951, Volumes I and II*. Minneapolis: University of Minnesota Press, 1951.

Harding, S. B. (ed.). *Indiana University, 1820–1904*. Bloomington: Indiana University, 1904.

Harper, C. *The Development of the Teachers College in the United States*. Bloomington, Ind.: McKnight and McKnight, 1935.

Harris, S. *A Statistical Portrait of Higher Education*. New York: McGraw-Hill, 1972.

Hauptman, A. "Trends in Federal and State Financial Commitment to Higher

Education." In D. H. Finifter, R. G. Baldwin, and J. R. Thelin, *The Uneasy Public Policy Triangle in Higher Education: Quality, Diversity, and Budgetary Efficiency*. New York: ACE/Oryx, 1991.

Hawkins, H. *Between Harvard and America*. New York: Oxford University Press, 1972.

Herrick, S. E. "Class of 1859," an address in memory of William Seymour Tyler, n.p.n.d.

Homer. *The Odyssey*. D.C.H. Riev, trans. London: Penguin Books, 1991.

"I Have A Dream Foundation." Brochure, I Have A Dream Foundation, New York, 1993.

Johnson, L. B. 200th Anniversary Convocation, Brown University, September 28, 1964.

Johnson, L. B. *Lyndon B. Johnson. Public Papers of the Presidents of the United States Containing the Public Messages, Speeches, and Statements of the President, 1963–64, Vol. I*. Washington, D.C.: United States Government Printing Office, 1965.

Kazin, A. *A Walker in the City*. San Diego: Harcourt Brace Jovanovich College Division, 1951.

King, S. *A History of Finances of Amherst College*. Amherst, Mass.: Amherst College Press, 1950.

Koos, L. *The Junior College*. Boston: Ginn, 1925.

Kotlowitz, A. *There Are No Children Here*. New York: Anchor Books, 1988.

Leslie, L., and Brinkman, P. *The Economic Value of Higher Education*. New York: Macmillan, 1988.

Levine, A. "The Longest Journey—Educating America's Underserved." In Proceedings of the 102nd Annual Meeting of the New England Association of Schools and Colleges, December 1987.

Levine, A. *A Dream Deferred: Higher Education for America's Poor*. Philadelphia: The Trustees of the University of Pennsylvania, 1989a.

Levine, A. *Shaping Higher Education's Future*. San Francisco: Jossey-Bass, 1989b.

Levine, D. O. *The American College and the Culture of Aspiration, 1915–1940*. Ithaca, N.Y.: Cornell University Press, 1986.

Lipset, S. M., and Riesman, D. *Education and Politics at Harvard: Two Essays Prepared for the Carnegie Commission on Higher Education*. New York: McGraw-Hill, 1975.

Lowery, G. R. "The Effect of Program Level Practices on Upward Bound Student Development: Student Selection, Instruction, Counseling, and College Placement," Cambridge, Mass.: Harvard Graduate School of Education, 1985.

Mabry, M. "The Ghetto Preppies," *Newsweek*, November 4, 1991.

Malcolm X (with assistance from Alex Haley). *The Autobiography of Malcolm X*. New York: Ballantine Books, 1992. (Originally published 1964.)

Monroe, S., and Goldman, P. *Brothers, Black and Poor*. New York: Ballantine Books, 1989.

Morison, S. E. *Harvard in the Seventeenth Century*. Cambridge, Mass.: Harvard University Press, 1936.

Mortenson, T. G. "Attitudes of Americans Toward Borrowing to Finance Educational Expenses 1959–1983." ACT Student Financial Aid Research Report Series. Iowa City, Iowa: American College Testing Program, 1988.

Mortenson, T. G. *Equity of Higher Education Opportunity for Women, Blacks, Hispanics and Low Income Students*. Iowa City, Iowa: ACT Student Financial Aid Research Report Series, January, 1991.

Mortenson, T. G. (ed.) "Postsecondary Education OPPORTUNITY: The Mortenson Report on Public Policy Analysis of Opportunity for Postsecondary Education, 1992–93." Iowa City, Iowa: Postsecondary Education Opportunity. January, February, and November, 1993.

Mortenson, T. G., and Wu, Z. *High School Graduation and College Participation of Young Adults by Family Income Backgrounds 1970 to 1989*. Iowa City, Iowa: American College Testing Program, September, 1990.

Mott, W. L. *Golden Multitudes: The Story of Best Sellers in the United States*. New York: Macmillan, 1947.

National Center for Education Statistics. *Projections of Educational Statistics to 2000*. Washington, D. C.: U. S. Department of Educational Research and Improvement, 1989.

National Commission on Excellence in Education. *A Nation at Risk: The Imperative for Educational Reform*. Washington, D. C.: Government Printing Office, 1983.

National Commission on Responsibilities for Financing Postsecondary Education. *Making College Affordable Again: Final Report*. Washington, D.C.: Government Printing Office, 1993.

P.L. 89–239, 79 stat. 1219. "The Higher Education Act of 1965."

Pangburn, J. *The Evolution of the American Teachers College*. New York: Teachers College, Columbia University, 1932.

Peckham, H. H. *The Making of the University of Michigan, 1817–1967*. Ann Arbor: University of Michigan Press, 1967.

Podell, J., and Anzovin, S. (eds.). *Speeches of the American Presidents*. New York: H. W. Wilson, 1988.

President's Commission on Higher Education. *Higher Education for American*

Democracy, Volumes I and II. New York: Harper and Brothers, Harper-Collins, 1947.

Reynolds, E. O. *The Social and Economic Status of College Students*. New York: Teachers College Press, 1927.

Richmond, G. "The Student Incentive Plan: Mitigating the Legacy of Poverty," *Phi Delta Kappan*, 1990, 72(3).

Riley, R. *Strong Families, Strong Schools: Building Community Partnerships for Learning*. Washington, D.C.: U.S. Department of Education, 1994.

Rosenblatt, R. *Children of War*. New York: Anchor Press, 1983.

Rudolph, F. *Mark Hopkins and the Log: Williams College 1836–1872*. New Haven, Conn.: Yale University Press, 1956.

Schnitzer, J. H. "Cognition, Reading and Society: An Analysis and Characterization of the Cognitive Abilities, Reading Behaviors, and Academic Skills of an Upward Bound Project." Cambridge, Mass.: Graduate School of Education, Harvard University, 1989.

Schorr, L. B. *Within Our Reach: Breaking the Cycle of Disadvantage*. New York: Anchor Books, 1988.

Simon, K. *Bronx Primitive: Portraits in a Childhood*. New York: HarperCollins, 1982.

Slosson, E. *Great American Universities*. New York: Macmillan, 1910.

Smith, D. C. *The First Century: A History of the University of Maine, 1865–1965*. Orono: University of Maine at Orono Press, 1972.

Solomon, B. M. *In the Company of Educated Women*. New Haven, Conn.: Yale University Press, 1985.

Story, R. *Harvard and the Boston Upper Class: The Forging of an Aristocracy*. Middletown, Conn.: Wesleyan University Press, 1980.

Thernstrom, S. In B. Bailyn, D. Fleming, O. Handlin, and S. Thernstrom, *Glimpses of the Harvard Past*. Cambridge, Mass.: Harvard University Press, 1986.

Tobias, M. *Old Dartmouth on Trial: The Transformation of the American Community in Nineteenth Century America*. New York: New York University Press, 1982.

U.S. Bureau of the Census. *Statistical Abstract of the U.S. 1990*. Washington, D.C.: U.S. Government Printing Office, 1990.

U.S. Bureau of the Census. *Current Population Reports*, Series P-60, "Poverty in the U.S.," Washington, D.C.: U.S. Government Printing Office, 1993.

Wilkerson, I. "Doing Whatever It Takes to Save a Child." *New York Times*, December 30, 1994, A1 and A10.

Wilson, W. J. *The Truly Disadvantaged: The Inner City, the Underclass and Public Policy*, Chicago: The University of Chicago Press, 1987.

Zweigenhaft, R. L., and Domhoff, G. W. *Blacks in the White Establishment?* New Haven, Conn.: Yale University Press, 1991.

Index